A PEACEFUL
New Year

A hope*books COLLABORATION

Introduction ©2025 Brian Dixon

Chapter One: So Much Joy Ahead: On Setting Intentions and Vision for the Year ©2025 by Natalie d'Aubermont Thompson

Chapter Two: Start with a Single Step: The Power of Celebrating Inch Stones ©2025 by Brianna Johnson

Chapter Three: Looking Within to Move Forward in Peace: Silencing the Inner Critic ©2025 by Rebecca McCartney

Chapter Four: Shedding the Old Way: Clothing Yourself with Christ in the New Year ©2025 by Jennifer Gorham

Chapter Five: Embracing Strength and Dignity for the New Year: Lessons from Habakkuk ©2025 by Rehana De Villiers

Chapter Six: Building a Firm Foundation: Achieving Better Health in the New Year and Beyond ©2025 by Lindsay Koach

Chapter Seven: When The Dark Night Lingers: Waking Up From Disillusion to Steadfast Hope ©2025 by Melissa Manion

Chapter Eight: Moving from Perplexed to Purposeful: Focusing on God's Plan ©2025 by Nancy Radloff

Chapter Nine: Grounded in Grace: How to Set Grace-Filled Goals When Life Happens ©2025 by Jess Henning

Chapter Ten: Letting Go: Moving Forward Unburdened ©2025 by Stephanie Gavel

Published by hope*books
2217 Matthews Township Pkwy
Suite D302
Matthews, NC 28105
www.hopebooks.com

hope*books is a division of hope*media

Printed in the United States of America

All rights reserved. Without limiting the rights under copyrights reserved above, no part of this publication may be scanned, uploaded, reproduced, distributed, or transmitted in any form or by any means whatsoever without express prior written permission from both the author and publisher of this book—except in the case of brief quotations embodied in critical articles and reviews.

Thank you for supporting the author's rights.

Paperback ISBN: 979-8-89185-300-3
Hardcover ISBN: 979-8-89185-144-3
Ebook ISBN: 979-8-89185-145-0
Library of Congress Number:2024950918

All Scripture quotations, unless otherwise indicated, are taken from the Holy Bible, New International Version®, NIV®. Copyright ©1973, 1978, 1984, 2011 by Biblica, Inc.™ Used by permission of Zondervan. All rights reserved worldwide. www.zondervan.comThe "NIV" and "New International Version" are trademarks registered in the United States Patent and Trademark Office by Biblica, Inc.™

Scripture quotations marked CSB have been taken from the Christian Standard Bible®, Copyright © 2017 by Holman Bible Publishers. Used by permission. Christian Standard Bible® and CSB® are federally registered trademarks of Holman Bible Publishers.

Scripture quotations marked ESV are from The ESV® Bible (The Holy Bible, English Standard Version®), © 2001 by Crossway, a publishing ministry of Good News Publishers. Used by permission. All rights reserved.

Scripture quotations taken from the (NASB®) New American Standard Bible®, Copyright © 1960, 1971, 1977, 1995, 2020 by The Lockman Foundation. Used by permission. All rights reserved. lockman.org"

Scripture quotations marked (NLT) are taken from the Holy Bible, New Living Translation, copyright ©1996, 2004, 2015 by Tyndale House Foundation. Used by permission of Tyndale House Publishers, Carol Stream, Illinois 60188. All rights reserved.

Table of Contents

Foreword vii

Introduction ix

Chapter 1
So Much Joy Ahead: On Setting Intentions
and Vision for the Year
By Natalie d'Aubermont Thompson 1

Chapter 2
Start with a Single Step: The Power
of Celebrating Inch Stones
By Brianna Johnson 17

Chapter 3
Looking Within to Move Forward in Peace:
Silencing the Inner Critic
By Rebecca McCartney, LCSW 33

Chapter 4
Shedding the Old Way: Clothing Yourself
with Christ in the New Year
By Jennifer Gorham, Psy.D. 51

Chapter 5
Embracing Strength and Dignity for the New Year:
Lessons from Habakkuk
By Rehana De Villiers 67

Chapter 6
Building a Firm Foundation: Achieving Better
Health in the New Year and Beyond
By *Lindsay Koach* 89

Chapter 7
When The Dark Night Lingers: Waking Up
From Disillusion to Steadfast Hope
By *Melissa Manion*..109

Chapter 8
Moving from Perplexed to Purposeful:
Focusing on God's Plan
By *Nancy Radloff* 121

Chapter 9
Grounded in Grace: How to Set Grace-Filled
Goals When Life Happens
By *Jess Henning*..135

Chapter 10
Letting Go: Moving Forward Unburdened
By *Stephanie Gavel*...159

About the Authors..169

Foreword

By Amanda McMullen

When one year ends and another begins, like many, my mind naturally drifts to improvement: *How do I make this year better than the last? How can I level up my body, mind, schedule, family, and finances? What things do I need to do or change to make this upcoming year the best year ever?* There is nothing wrong with thinking this way. My performance-oriented brain is simply wired to plan, to look ahead, to optimize. But what if this year, God is calling us to something deeper than achieving more, doing more, being more? What if He is after something much more important than the items on our to-accomplish list or our resolutions and goals? Maybe this year, the "more" the Lord wants to give us is *peace*.

As the editor of A *Peaceful New Year*, I have been challenged by these ten amazing authors to think a little bit differently about my plans. They encourage us to trade in our striving and uncover God's purposes for our year and, ultimately, our lives. We learn to lay aside drivenness and clothe ourselves with gentleness instead—toward ourselves and toward others. These authors show us that in order to move forward, we must do the deep work of seeing ourselves as God sees us—and seeing Him as He really is, not as our minds have conceived of Him. As we move into a new year or any new season of life, we have to show ourselves kindness and grace when "life happens" or even when it falls apart. If you take from these chapters, I have no doubt you will find yourself more aligned with who God has made you to be and living from a place of wholeness—body, soul, mind, and spirit—in the coming year and beyond.

I am incredibly proud of the work these authors have done to share these stories, testimonies, and teachings with you. These ten women have poured forth beautiful wisdom from the heart and from hard-earned experience and years walking with God. May their hope-filled words be a gift to you as you prepare for the year ahead, and may you start your new year with the peace that comes from knowing Jesus and trusting in His commitment to making you whole.

Introduction

Welcome to A *Peaceful New Year*—a collection of stories and insights designed to help you start the year with intention, renewal, and grace. At Hope*Books, we believe the new year offers a unique opportunity to reflect on where we've been, envision where we're going, and embrace the rest and peace God calls us to.

This book is more than just a guide to resolutions; it's an invitation to step away from the relentless striving and step into a season of purpose and hope. Each chapter is filled with heartfelt wisdom from incredible authors who share their personal experiences, spiritual reflections, and practical tools to help you embrace rest, celebrate progress, and live intentionally in the year ahead.

From learning to silence your inner critic and celebrating "inch stones" to setting grace-filled goals and moving forward unburdened, the stories in these pages will inspire and equip you to approach the new year with clarity and peace. Together, these voices form a beautiful tapestry of faith, resilience, and hope.

As you read, may you find encouragement to slow down, reflect deeply, and begin this new year with a heart full of trust in God's promises. My prayer is that this book becomes a companion on your journey to embrace rest, renewal, and a life rooted in His grace.

Brian Dixon

Learn About Each Chapter from the Authors:

In Natalie d'Aubermont Thompson's chapter, "So Much Joy Ahead: On Setting Intentions and Vision for the Year," the author shares what living seasonally means to her family and how casting a vision and setting intentions, not goals, is a more realistic, and ultimately hopeful, framework for life. This chapter will encourage the reader to set aside time in January for reflection and also glean some tangible ideas for what Natalie and her family do to cast vision, set intentions, and celebrate seasons.

Brianna Johnson's chapter, "Start with a Single Step: The Power of Celebrating Inch Stones," explores the importance of breaking down big goals into smaller, manageable steps she calls inch stones. Drawing from her personal experiences as a perfectionist and as a special needs mom, Brianna illustrates how celebrating these small, incremental achievements can lead to lasting progress and joy. By embracing imperfection, focusing on growth, and finding meaning in the smallest wins, she encourages readers to shift their mindset from chasing milestones to appreciating the journey itself.

In Rebecca McCartney's chapter, "Looking Within to Move Forward in Peace: Silencing the Inner Critic," she shares from a therapist's perspective the reasons we often have difficulty creating the change we desire. Rebecca explains the ways your inner critic makes it challenging to begin, gain momentum, and follow through on your goals. With humor and real examples, she gives the reader practical tools to silence her inner critic and achieve the changes she desires this new year.

Introduction

In Jennifer Gorham's chapter "Shedding the Old Way: Clothing Yourself with Christ in the New Year," she gives us a fresh perspective on New Year's resolutions. Her integration of Paul's descriptions of God's armor and being clothed in gentleness reorients our focus toward relationships instead of achievements. Through her personal and professional experience, she shares how our identity as God's beloved leads us to be gentle with ourselves and others.

Rehana De Villiers' chapter, "Embracing Strength and Dignity for the New Year: Lessons from Habakkuk," helps Christian women face life's challenges with practical steps and lessons from the Old Testament book of Habakkuk. She shares five key insights to start the new year with strength, dignity, deeper faith, and less striving. Using her own story of unmet expectations and struggles beyond her control, Rehana shows how doubts and despair can lead to a stronger trust in God. Her chapter encourages readers to lean on God's promises and find renewed hope.

In Lindsay Koach's chapter, "Building a Firm Foundation: Achieving Better Health in the New Year and Beyond," Lindsay provides a different perspective when it comes to New Year's health and wellness resolutions. Transitioning from a goal-setting mindset to a more reflective, support-oriented, and holistic approach to renewing health, Lindsay delves into the intricacies of laying the necessary groundwork before taking action on health and wellness goals. Widening the scope on what being healthy really means, Lindsay sets her reader on a path toward long-term health and well-being. She equips her readers with knowledge and insight that will support them through achieving better health in the new year and beyond.

A Peaceful New Year

In Melissa Manion's chapter, "When The Dark Night Lingers: Waking Up From Disillusion to Steadfast Hope," she takes you on a perilous but necessary journey to the foundation of your belief. She shares with raw vulnerability how God allowed everything to fall apart so He could put her back together soundly. If you have ever found yourself wondering if somehow you have been forgotten or overlooked by God, her story will remind you that you are not alone in that query. Most importantly, without being trite, she reminds you that despite what your eyes may see, you are never far from His unwavering and relentless love.

In Nancy Radloff's chapter, "Moving from Perplexed to Purposeful: Focusing on God's Plan," you will be affirmed knowing that you are created, redeemed, and empowered by God for God's planned purpose. With engaging stories and examples, Nancy lays out a framework for you to discover your God-given "GTAs" and "orbits" in living out what God has planned for you to do for a time such as this.

In Jess Henning's chapter, "Grounded in Grace: How to Set Grace-Filled Goals When Life Happens," she explores the challenges we face when life throws us unexpected curveballs, leaving our goals seemingly out of reach. Through personal stories and practical advice, she shares how to set meaningful and flexible goals, allowing room for grace during life's most difficult seasons. Jess encourages readers to embrace their season, redefine success, and approach goal-setting with self-compassion. Her chapter offers valuable insights on navigating unexpected changes without abandoning the dreams that matter most.

Introduction

In Stephanie Gavel's chapter, "Letting Go: Moving Forward Unburdened," you will learn to live unburdened by the past that threatens to keep you stuck. Even though we all long to live a life unencumbered, we get tripped up from time to time, entangled by past mistakes, words left unsaid, fears too weighty to be said aloud, and feelings that we struggle to fully identify. It can suffocate and imprison us from within. Through her inspiring words, Stephanie encourages us that it is possible to move forward!

Chapter 1

So Much Joy Ahead: On Setting Intentions and Vision for the Year

By Natalie d'Aubermont Thompson

"SO BE TRULY GLAD. THERE IS WONDERFUL JOY AHEAD."
—1 PETER 1:6A NLT

A Changing Landscape

I lift my gaze from my laptop, and my eyes feast on the blaze of autumn foliage in Michigan. Rich auburns mingle with oak yellows and evergreens. The air is ripe with the crisp smell of apples and bonfires, and I smile at the pumpkins and colorful mums dotting the neighborhood stoops. As a family, we are finally settling into our school and work routines while embracing the beauty of a Midwestern fall: squeezing in apple picking and corn mazes between soccer games and ballet practices.

After a decade of living here, I know that soon this landscape will drastically change. In a smattering of weeks, it'll either be a hushed wonderland with winter sunlight dazzling off the snow or bare branches laden with icy rain under ominous gray skies. Driveways will reveal slush some days, while bright plastic sleds and snow shovels make their appearances on others.

I start to prepare now—I spot gloves and snowsuits on sale at Costco and grab several for our rapidly growing hands and legs. I ensure our mudroom is well-supplied with boots and colorful wool hats. I dig out our favorite soup recipes and make sure our pantry is stocked with ingredients for hearty meals. Our firewood box is brought upstairs to the living room, and I find myself looking forward to those cozy evenings hearthside: reading aloud, playing games, or watching movies snuggled together.

Internally, however, I sense a current of anxiety beneath the surface—an anxiety about the coming holidays. Yes, I cherish the lovely parts, but there's also an underlying sense of need and greed. The frantic scheduling of recitals, school exams, and the final push to wrap up year-end professional projects loom over us. Not to mention the parental expectations to make the season 'magical' for everyone—all within budget, of course.

And honestly, a bit of dread creeps in for the New Year. Amidst my desire to be intentional during Advent, to quiet myself and prepare room, there's an assumption that by January 1st, I MUST have goals outlined and ready to implement. If I don't, I'm left with a feeling of inadequacy—emotionally, professionally, financially. Why don't we have a trip booked for spring break? Why can't I lose those stubborn ten pounds? How will I just get through a long winter emotionally intact?

And for those of us in midlife, there's the sobering question: is there really anything to look forward to anymore? The anticipatory grief of a year that falls short of our hopes and dreams is real, robbing us of joy in planning for what could be.

A Bit of Context

Confession time: I used to be one of those goal-setters. A natural achiever and planner, I gravitated towards goals and relished knowing what was coming next. Having kids, however, has challenged this. Having three kids—each with their own personalities and giftings—I find myself navigating not only my own expectations but also those of my family.

In this chapter, I hope to share my journey and offer ideas on how to mindfully set intentions, rather than rigid goals, for a new year. Together, we can create a unique vision for ourselves and our families, given the seasons of a year and life.

For context, I grew up as the second of five children in an immigrant family. I felt the pressure of my parents' sacrifices weighing on my academic shoulders and rose to the occasion, graduating with honors from Tufts University and later the London School of Economics and Political Science. When I met the man who would become my husband in Washington, D.C., I was deeply immersed in studying for the LSAT and applying for degrees in International Relations, all while working at a top research consulting firm. I remember telling him I had a five-year plan, and I wasn't sure it left much time for dating. I must credit him for not running away; if anything, my drive for achievement piqued his curiosity as it matched his own.

For a time, our efforts bore fruit: we pursued degrees at top institutions, lived in London, worked at prestigious financial and legal firms, and invested in friendships and service to our local churches—be it in D.C., Durham, NC, London, or Ann Arbor, MI. Then, as babies arrived, I decided to leave the corporate world to start my own consulting and executive leadership company, allowing me to work on my own timeline. Yet I felt torn between the world of young children, where I was constantly admonished to 'enjoy every moment, it goes so fast,' and the desire to continue my professional journey.

In less than five years, I made an international move and then two domestic ones, resulting in three babies born in three different states. I set up a company and served as board chair of a nonprofit. Yet, despite all this, I felt inadequate. I look back now and realize how much I bought into the hustle culture of the 2010s: #girlboss, 'make it happen,' and 'girl, wash your face' became normalized monikers. Setting goals and pushing myself to achieve them without considering much of my vocational calling became my default way of life. While being driven isn't inherently bad, pursuing it out of a sense of inadequacy leads to fear-based behavior, not freedom.

As I emerged from the chaos of those baby and toddler years, parenting young children so close in age challenged my high-paced modus operandi. Their fascination with examining frogs in mud, delight in spring crocuses, and pure joy in a pile of picture books opened a part of my heart that had long been dormant. It was then that my life adage became 'cultivating wonder.'

On Vision

I mention this background to illustrate how we began to intentionally approach our family vision. When our children were little (around five and younger), we honestly didn't include them much in our discussions about family vision; during that season, most parents are simply trying to keep up with the physical and emotional demands of each developmental stage. However, something shifts around age five or six, when you begin to see your child's character emerge and their schedules start to merge with yours. Education, whether at school or home, comes to the forefront, and for some parents, formal faith training begins to take shape around this time, while others see practices for sports or the arts popping up on the calendar.

There's relief in this predictability, but as any parent knows, the 'blank space' on the calendar, once filled with naps and park visits, can quickly become cluttered with birthday parties, sports games, church programs, and more. When we started feeling these growing pains, we knew it was time to establish a family rhythm and routine—one that was flexible enough to accommodate the changes that come with children. This also sparked discussions about our family culture. My husband and I began this conversation organically, but it's worth engaging in whether your kids are little or older.[1]

---

[1] I highly recommend *The Cloistered Away Podcast* (host Bethany Douglass) on Spotify for insights on developing a family culture.

Some helpful questions we used for this exercise included:

- What do we want to be about as a family?
- What makes our family unique?
- What do we value most?
- How do we want our kids to remember what was special about our family?

You don't have to craft a formal mission statement, but if you choose to, it can serve as a guiding reference regardless of what a year brings, allowing it to evolve as your children grow. We really fleshed this out during the 2020 pandemic when, given the circumstances, we had more time for reflection on who we are as a family (our kids were aged 5-10 at the time). We used a workshop approach with easels, post-its, and dry-erase markers, brainstorming adjectives that represented our values, which we distilled into a phrase: *Live well with the Word in the world.*

As our kids grew, we began including them in our yearly family vision, helping them set individual goals. Yes, it's more than fine to use the word 'goal' as long as it's not the overall metric! The aim is to guide them toward cultivating intentional and faithful living, both as a family and individually, as I steward three souls. My friend Christy Ogden, who leads Field and Fold, an organization that prepares people for different life stages, shared with me: "*We have found so much help in setting vision for our family of seven each year. With a lot of different agendas, schedules, and personalities in our family, setting a clear vision helps us know what to pursue, say yes to, and how to guide any decisions we need to make. It gives us purpose and clarity for moving forward.*"

However, before getting into the details, it's important to note that *there is nothing magical about January 1st*. As a parent, December tends to be busy with all the celebrations, but it's also Advent—a time my faith tradition implores me to slow down, listen, and actively await. It's about a manger, a weary world rejoicing, a silent night. Over time, I've given myself permission to rest in the joyful anticipation of what is here and now and what is to come. Living in an area with distinct seasons, I also have found winter to be my most introspective time. As Katherine May, author of *Wintering* reflects: "Winter is a time of withdrawing from the world, maximizing scant resources, carrying out acts of brutal efficiency, and vanishing from sight; but that's where transformation occurs. Winter is not the death of the life cycle, but its crucible."[2] By releasing the pressures of a January 1st deadline, I can use January—a calm port after the holiday storm—to reflect on my passions, callings, and interests, aligning them both vocally and personally.

Bringing Life to Vision

At some point in January (it can be any time during the month), my husband and I meet to go over our roles and goals. We use a few simple templates that guide us through questions about rhythms and schedules for the season, helping us live intentionally while prayerfully taking inventory of the year.[3] At times we've done this together. Other times, we've each done this separately before meeting to compare notes.

---

[2] May, Katherine. *Wintering: The Power of Rest and Retreat in Difficult Times*. Riverhead Books, 2020.

[3] Author note: I would like to credit the work of Antioch Community Church as well as Allen, Jennie. *Dream Guide: A 40-Day Journey to Discover God's Dream for You*. WaterBrook, 2021.

No exact formula—either works! Some years, we've planned ahead for childcare to do this over a weekend; other years, we've met at a coffee shop or at home. I find it helpful for each of us to have our personal and work calendars—both digital and paper—along with any other relevant calendars for the kids (school, sports, youth group, etc.) to plan logistically while being vulnerable about our dreams.

While this process takes time (and can sometimes unearth wounds related to unfulfilled dreams, so be ready for some soul work!), it truly sets a vision for the year. Helpful reflection questions include: *What am I moving toward, and what am I ready to leave behind? What am I praying for spiritually, mentally, physically, financially, etc.?* Dreams and hopes naturally ebb and flow in different seasons, but taking the time to write them down, think about goals—whether they are Everest-sized or short-term—and process them with trusted ones can be invaluable.

In the end, I'm always glad I take the time to meditate on my hopes, goals, and dreams for the new year. I confess there's always a part of me that fears putting certain dreams on paper—promises unfulfilled—but I know that is part of the faith journey: to hope in the unseen and trust that our boundaries have indeed fallen in pleasant places. As author James K.A. Smith reflects, "An eschatological life is one animated by the cadences of two hopeful exhortations: lift up your hearts and be not afraid."[4]

On Progress

Another exercise that we tend to include at the beginning of the year is 'Word of the Year.' I started that years ago before

---

[4] Smith, James K.A. *How to Inhabit Time: Understanding the Past, Facing the Future, Living Faithfully Now.* Brazos Press, 2022.

children, but as ours grew older, it has been fun to do this with them, to see them pray for what they believe God has in store for them or perhaps an area of their life they want to intentionally focus on. Their words have ranged from *courage* to *passionate* to *renewal* and *core*. If you are able to take the time to find a Scripture verse or quote to tie in with it, that certainly makes it richer, but it is not necessary. Just finding the quiet time to pray for your word and share it with one another is so special.

As the year unfolds, we can look back on the tangible achievements—goals met, projects completed, and milestones reached. These accomplishments can serve as markers of growth and progress, whether in personal development, family life, or professional endeavors. Also, bringing children into this and spending time envisioning what you'd like to do at various times of the year as a family is a great way to embrace the seasons. As I said, living in Michigan has taught me to appreciate the days in front of me as they change quickly, and the next thing I know, we're in a new season, literally or figuratively.

What this looks like is each quarter, we take the large Post-It Sticky Easel Pad and have our kids brainstorm things they are anticipating: in the summer, this can be time at the lake, hosting out-of-town family, cherry picking; in the winter, it can look like ice skating, hot cocoa movie nights and making blessing bags for the unhoused in our community. It is also fun for us to add things like read-aloud books or special traditions, such as the local Turkey Trot. We purposely steer away from the term 'bucket list,' as that term felt self-serving, so using names like 'Spring Fling,' 'Sun Fun,'

'Awesome Autumn,' and 'Winter WonderFun' make it unique to our family. As the kids have gotten older and more involved in their own communities, their sports tournaments and theatrical performances are added in. This all serves to add flavor to our family culture, and we tie in gratitude by taking time to go over the Post-It notes and be thankful for what we were able to experience together (or adding in new things that happened spontaneously) as we transition to a new one. Apart from cultivating gratitude, I feel that this exercise is helpful for me to not get overwhelmed in certain seasons but to appreciate them all in their own way.

Reflection and Rest

Another thing we do to mark the end of an academic year is a special breakfast to celebrate the milestones and memories. We refer to it as our 'debrief breakfast,' and we do it to bring closure to the formal academic year (we've done this in seasons of homeschool as well as traditional school), and it's wonderful to teach kids the importance of reflection on both their character and accomplishments. Some years, that accomplishment can look like trying out a new sport or persevering with an instrument that was challenging; for another, it's mastering a subject matter like multiplication. As parents, it's a chance to speak life into them (for example, I noticed you grew in patience toward your brother, or I saw you bravely navigate a few school/sport, or you handled a tricky friend dynamic very well this year). Individually and as a family, some questions we make sure to ask are:

- Where did you grow?
- What worked? What didn't?

- What was a highlight? What was hard/challenging?
- What are you looking forward to this summer? What are you eager to do, to try?

A reminder: it's perfectly okay to reiterate and revise as the year progresses. *Revision* is one of my favorite words; it's not about starting over but about resetting and reclaiming a vision crafted for a reason. Seasons will come and go just as they do in life, helping us live liturgically. Morgan Harper Nichols writes, "*In the same way there is a rhythm to nature, I have rhythms too.*"[5] Cal Newport, in *Slow Productivity*, affirms that this pattern exists in our professional lives as well: "To work without change or rest all year would have seemed unusual to most of our ancestors. Seasonality was deeply integrated into the human experience."[6]

If I have thoughtfully prayed for a vision for the year, I'm more apt to anticipate the seasons of hard work and when to allow time for rest. Leaning into these seasons without fear or anxiety is not easy, especially for those of us juggling children and aging parents, but it's possible by mindfully taking stock of what is in front of you and knowing when to prune and when to reap and harvest. For me, mindfulness correlates strongly with attention, and as the poet Drew Jackson notes: "Attention is the doorway to wonder."[7]

It's also crucial to acknowledge the goals that remain unfulfilled. These missed opportunities can lead to feelings of disappointment or frustration. However, they also pro-

---

[5] Nichols, Morgan Harper. *Peace is a Practice: An Invitation to Breathe Deep and Find a New Rhythm for Life.* Zondervan Books, 2022.

[6] Newport, Cal. *Slow Productivity.* Portfolio, 2024.

[7] Jackson, Drew. [@d.jacksonpoetics] "Attention is the doorway to wonder." Instagram, 14 September 2024, https://www.instagram.com/d.jacksonpoetics/p/C_5bq0jx-cO/

vide fertile ground for reflection and learning—what hindered progress, and how can we adjust our expectations moving forward? Despite the ups and downs, a steady sense of purpose can be a guiding light throughout the year. This overarching purpose helps us remain focused, reminding us of our values and the vision we set out to achieve, even when specific goals shift or change. Each experience—both success and failure—offers invaluable lessons. Taking time to reflect on these moments allows us to gain insights that can shape our future intentions. This reflection cultivates resilience and adaptability, reinforcing the idea that growth often emerges from challenges. Each breath, every opportunity, and all our relationships are gifts from God. This understanding calls us to live with gratitude and intentionality, honoring the gifts bestowed upon us.

On Unexpected Turns

Life is dynamic, and our intentions must remain flexible. Adjusting our goals in response to life's changes allows us to stay aligned with our purpose and calling. We have to tread lightly here as it's easy to let our goals overshadow our relationship with God. When our intentions become the focal point, we risk losing sight of the Divine presence guiding our journey. Our intentions should serve as efforts to listen and embrace the path He has set for us. Keeping God at the center ensures that our pursuits align with His greater plan. We also have to remember to hold all these goals and intentions loosely and to build rest into the process as well. Just as there are seasons to harvest, there are seasons to lay fallow. As Tricia Hersey implores us to remember: "You were not just born to center your entire existence on work and labor.

You were born to heal, to grow, to be of service to yourself and community, to practice, to experiment, to create, to have space, to dream, and to connect."[8]

Also, as we all know, despite our best-laid plans and visions, life will inevitably present conflict, difficulties, and even unfair suffering. Job losses, new relationships, or unexpected opportunities can derail our plans. These detours, while challenging, can also lead to new paths we might never have considered. Tragedy, illness, or the loss of loved ones can profoundly impact our intentions. Such experiences invite deep reflection and may reshape our vision entirely, calling us to reevaluate what truly matters.

Several years ago, together with his siblings, my husband helped his aging parents downsize his childhood home in the spring and, in the summer, moved them into assisted living near his sister (so now they were four hours from us instead of 45 min away). Later that fall, our beautiful niece tragically died by suicide. In January of that new year, we tried to do our visioning as we know deep down how important it is, but when we reflected on the year and got to the part entitled 'What to grieve,' I saw the list of losses grow longer and longer and could not bear it. We were in a cafe, and I had to excuse myself to weep in the restroom before proceeding further. We made a bit of progress that day but ultimately decided to be gentle with ourselves and table the rest of the conversation for later.

As you can imagine, it didn't outwardly look like a productive time of visioning, but it reminded me of how important it is to name the losses to grieve them one by one before

---

[8] Hersey, Tricia. *Rest is Resistance: A Manifesto*. Little, Brown Spark, 2022.

moving into vision planning. My personality is not built that way—I am reflective but forward-thinking by nature, and nothing jazzes me more than future plans, goals, or dreams. And while I didn't walk away with the 'to-do' list I wanted, I know that the time wasn't wasted and that even the tears would be rich compost to till for future planning soil. We ended up meeting again a few weeks later and tentatively began to make plans and voice our hopes and dreams. I say this to encourage anyone who is tired of the well-meaning but, frankly, toxic positivity that can float around the ether these days. A new year doesn't erase all the grief that came with the prior, but it does allow us a chance to offer up hopes and dreams, prayers for healing, and a season of flourishing for ourselves and our loved ones.

Holding On To Hope

As we navigate the beauty and complexity of family life, let's hold onto hope, waiting expectantly for what the new year will bring while remaining deeply anchored in the present. Scripture reminds us in 1 Peter that despite trials, there is wonderful joy ahead. But then there is also the waiting. My former pastor Bryan Gregory once reminded us in an Advent series of the idea that "waiting is an act of hope..a deliberate act of faith even in the midst of the pain and the trauma. It requires a decision to lean forward toward hope and to believe that waiting itself will bear fruit." In doing so, we open ourselves up to the fullness of life, finding joy in the moments that truly matter and becoming more attuned to the rhythms that shape our family's story. It's essential to remember that the purpose of setting intentions is not to achieve everything on our own. Rather, it's about recognizing our dependence on a higher power and the community around us. Our journey is rooted in the practice of waiting and hoping, reflecting a profound trust in the unfolding of God's plan for us.

Chapter 2

Start with a Single Step: The Power of Celebrating Inch Stones

By Brianna Johnson

"YOUR BEGINNINGS WILL SEEM HUMBLE, SO PROSPEROUS WILL YOUR FUTURE BE." —JOB 8:7

Have you ever opened a fresh planner and thought about all the things that you'll do differently this year? Me too. There's something about a blank page that I find exciting and inspiring. But that new planner has never actually made me a different person. Maybe you've noticed that too.

Those grand plans go well for a few weeks, and then something happens, and you take a step backward, or two. As the momentum slows and eventually stops, you're disappointed and possibly blaming yourself for falling into an old pattern—the exact one you were trying to replace. That's what I do.

The Trap of Perfectionism

You see, I'm a perfectionist. Well, I used to be. I'm working on that. I used to start something new and expect that I'd be an expert within the first few times of doing that new thing. Sometimes it happens, but most often it doesn't. When it doesn't happen, and I don't feel like I'm going to excel at the task or activity, I won't do it. For me, perfectionism looks like procrastination. I'll tell myself that it's research, or prepping, or planning, or learning, but really, it's me being afraid of doing something wrong.

I don't like being wrong. Not that I know anyone who does. Mistakes are embarrassing, but that's just my pride talking. Here's the thing about embarrassment—it's not fatal and it's not permanent. It's uncomfortable, it's less than ideal, but it will pass. If I look back on the experiences that have taught me the most, there are usually mistakes involved. Embracing the idea that something good can come from a mistake has helped me take messy and imperfect action in a lot of areas of my life.

There's something freeing about acknowledging that things can be adjusted. Very few things any of us do are going to be set in stone or will be a one-and-done kind of activity. Instead of approaching the things I create and do with judgment, I try to approach them with curiosity. Where can this be better? How can this be easier? Can I make this more fun? I've learned that one of the kindest things I can do for myself is to allow myself the luxury of being a beginner. How did I learn that? My son.

Lessons from My Son: Embracing a Different Timeline

I have three amazing boys—Walter, Oscar, and Arthur. They're all unique, and they teach me every day. I'm blessed to be their mom, and I can't wait to see what they do as they grow. Walter is our oldest, and when he was a little over a year old, he was diagnosed with a rare genetic condition, Bainbridge Ropers Syndrome. At the time, there were only 150 people globally who shared his BRS diagnosis—now we're a community of about 300 people and their families. The diagnosis means that he deals with a variety of delays compared to his typical peers. Some are physical, some are cognitive, some are emotional and social.

When Walter was little, we would look for all the milestones that new parents talk about—when he would roll over, when he would sit up, when he would start walking, when he would say his first words, etc. Some of those milestones didn't happen for a long time. He took his first steps when he was four. Some of those milestones still haven't happened. Walter is nonverbal for now, so we haven't heard his first words. We've heard his voice plenty, though, and it's wonderful.

Reframing Guilt and Letting Go of Control

At first, it was easy to get concerned or discouraged that things weren't happening when they were "supposed to." Remember those perfectionist tendencies I mentioned? It was impossible not to blame myself for the delays. Clearly, I must have done something wrong, or he wouldn't be struggling like this. Clearly, I needed to do something more to get him the support he needed.

That kind of guilt weighs you down. Especially because it's both unnecessary and untrue. That guilt is sneaky, too. It starts off as genuine curiosity, but the judgment creeps in. Instead of asking, "How can this be better," it's "How can I be better?" Or "How can I be that bad at something?" It's that little voice in the back of your mind that assumes you can control things that you really can't and then blames you when they don't go how you wanted.

That little voice is a liar. It can be hard in the moment when something goes wrong, but you have to look at the situation and really ask whether you could have changed the outcome. If you did all you could do, you did enough. That guilt, that fear, is really there to protect you. Your brain doesn't want you to feel pain or discomfort, so it pushes you to avoid situations that will cause those feelings.

As a special needs mom, I don't get to avoid some of those situations. Complicated medical procedures, conversations with doctors where we don't agree on the approach to take for him, advocating for him with the team at school, answering well-meaning but sometimes offensive questions. My need to protect myself extends to him, and often, it would just be easier to stay home in our little bubble. Easier, but not better.

I ask a lot of questions, especially of myself. Over time, the question I'd ask shifted from "What did I do wrong that he deserves this?" to "What did I do RIGHT that I deserve HIM?" I bet you can feel the difference. That shift didn't happen overnight. Walter is nine as I write this, and it took the better part of those nine years for me to consistently be at that place. I still have days when I'm angry at the seeming unfairness of it all, but those are rare now.

The Shift from Milestones to Inch Stones

So what changed? We stopped waiting for Walter's milestones. They'll happen when they're supposed to, when the timing is right for him. Not my plan—but it never really is, is it? Instead, we started to embrace the little things that reminded us that slowly moving forward is still moving forward.

Walter took five steps, then ten, then he walked down the driveway, and then he used the steps to get on the school bus all on his own. Even his bus driver cried happy tears that day. The video of him doing it that we shared on Facebook reminded us how many people are cheering him on and cheering us on, too.

We celebrate everything. The first jump, the first clear communication, the first laugh at a real joke, the first game played, the first time a marker is used correctly and the cap put back on—sure, that drawing was on the wall, but it came off... mostly.

Seeing the impact small steps have on the way he learns new skills has challenged the way I approach things for myself. What if I don't have to get it right the first time? What if I allow myself the chance to learn, practice, and improve over time? Sometimes, when we're teaching our kids, we need to learn the lessons too.

Building a Plan That Works for You

That's the approach I'm taking now. Instead of looking at what I want to change for the coming year and expecting that I'll be able to start and maintain it all on January 1st, I think in terms of where I want to be by December 31st. Then

I work backward. I love a plan. Often, at work, I have a deadline in mind and then work back to build the plan to make it happen. Occasionally, that means I have to have awkward conversations about when we can realistically expect a new hire to start or an email campaign to launch, but that's part of planning.

So why had I never considered doing that for myself? I don't have a good answer for that. It's probably some sort of unconscious trick to stay safe and in my comfort zone because the lizard parts of my brain would rather deal with the frustration of staying in the same place with the same expectations than face the unknown fears that come with making an actual change.

That's why I'm replacing the big fear with small celebrations. The excitement is something to look forward to and it definitely helps with the motivation I need to keep going.

You may be thinking that setting a plan for the year could be really hard. It could be, but it doesn't have to be. Here are a few things that I've done to get myself to a bigger goal.

- If you want to build up to being able to hold a plank position for 5 minutes, start at 30 seconds, then 45 seconds, then 1 minute, and go up from there. You can spend a few days at each specific timeframe, and then by the end of 30 days, you're at your 5-minute goal. Pinterest is a great resource for this kind of plan.
- If you want to read a book like *Anna Karenina*, don't plan to read the whole thing in one sitting or even one month. Commit to one chapter each day. They're actually short chapters, so this is very doable. By November, you're done.

- If you want to reorganize or repaint your entire house, pick one room or one closet to start with. Pick a place where you spend a lot of time so you can enjoy the changes sooner. I sleep better when our bedroom is clear, and I work with better focus when my office is tidy.

Shifting from focusing on big, high-level goals to the smaller steps that lead to them is like zooming in with a camera lens. At the high level, you see the whole picture—the end vision or destination you want to reach. But that big vision can sometimes feel overwhelming or abstract because it's distant and complex. By shifting your focus to the smaller, actionable steps, you break down that larger goal into manageable pieces, giving yourself a clearer path forward.

This shift helps you move from dreaming about the outcome to planning the process. It's about identifying the key milestones, habits, and actions required to make progress day by day. It also brings a sense of momentum as you start to accomplish smaller tasks and see tangible progress, which reinforces motivation. Each small step becomes a building block, and before you know it, those incremental actions accumulate and bring you closer to the larger vision. Essentially, it transforms an ambitious goal from something daunting into a series of achievable actions that gradually lead you toward success. I call these smaller steps "inch stones."

The Power of Inch Stones: Small Wins, Big Impact

You might be wondering, what exactly is an inch stone? It's a term I love because it represents the many small steps that add up over time to help you reach the bigger milestones that make up your goals. We often hear about and share milestones, but inch stones are the quiet, steady achievements that come before. They're the tiny victories that might seem insignificant on their own but, when stacked together, build the foundation for meaningful and lasting change.

Think of inch stones like the small, regular pebbles that pave a long road. Each one may not seem like much by itself, but together, they create the path that leads you to where you want to go. Each small step may not feel monumental, but it's a part of the journey and deserves to be celebrated.

The beauty of inch stones is that they give you permission to acknowledge progress even when the bigger milestone feels far away. They help build momentum and keep you motivated, reminding you that every bit of effort counts. In our family, we celebrate inch stones all the time—whether it's Walter taking a few more steps than the day before, Oscar trying a new food, or Arthur remembering to put his toys away. These inch stones are worth noticing because they add up to something amazing over time, turning what might feel like a slow crawl into steady, meaningful growth.

By focusing on inch stones, you shift from worrying about how much farther you have to go to appreciating how far you've already come. And that shift makes all the difference in helping you keep going, even when progress feels slow.

It takes time to learn a new skill or build a new habit. As you build out your plan, decide what timing is best for you. Can you reach your goal in 30 days, 60 days, 90 days, or will it take all year? There's no right answer. That was hard for me to learn and accept. I was a straight-A student starting in kindergarten—I love having the right answer. You may find that you think you need more or less time than what you originally planned, and it's ok to adjust along the way.

Think about the things you have planned throughout your year as well. I know that over the summer, when all three boys are home, I'm going to be spending more time with them than I will on home projects or getting into new things for work. I've tried before to keep going at my school year pace, and it only leaves me frustrated. The whole point of this approach is to minimize frustration. Think about the times of the year that you know are busy for you, and try to schedule as little as you can for them.

You'll also want to decide how you'll celebrate each inch stone as you achieve it. Small achievements are still achievements. They stack up over time. It's like the old saying that a journey of a thousand miles starts with a single step. Is that first step a cause for celebration? How about the hundredth step? Your celebrations don't have to look and feel a certain way; just what works for you.

For example, if you want to run a half marathon, do you celebrate with new running shoes after your first 5k? If you want to finally clean out the junk in your basement, do you repaint the room and refresh the space with new furniture when you're done? Do you go out with your spouse or your friends when you get halfway to where you're headed? Maybe a new notebook and a beautiful pen will help you get excited about your new journaling habit.

Finding Joy in the Journey

The beauty of these small celebrations is that they allow you to actively choose to have more joy in your life. Happiness is a feeling—it doesn't last. But joy is a choice. It sets the tone for how you look at and interact with your world. I'm not trying to promote toxic positivity or anything that isn't genuine, but if you look for things to celebrate and be excited about, you'll find them every time.

Choose Joy

Happiness and joy are often used interchangeably, but they are different in nature. Happiness is a fleeting emotion that depends on external events or circumstances. It comes from moments like winning a prize, receiving a compliment, or enjoying a good meal. However, because it relies on what's happening around you, happiness is temporary. It rises and falls, much like a wave, and can disappear as quickly as it arrives when things take a turn for the worse.

Joy, on the other hand, is a deeper, more stable sense of contentment that comes from within. Unlike happiness, joy isn't tied to circumstances. It's a choice—a way of seeing and responding to the world that allows you to find meaning even during difficult times. You can experience joy by focusing on gratitude, purpose, and connection, regardless of external challenges. In this way, joy is more like a lighthouse, offering steady light and direction, even in life's storms.

The distinction between happiness and joy is important because happiness, though pleasant, is short-lived. If you spend your life chasing happiness, you may feel disappointed when life doesn't go as planned. Joy, however, can change the way you approach life for the better. It allows you to find beauty and hope in imperfect moments and respond with grace, optimism, and love. Cultivating joy builds resilience, helping you navigate challenges with an inner sense of peace and meaning that endures no matter what life brings.

Celebrate the Highs and Embrace the Lows

When we look around, it's sometimes hard to see past the struggles, the conflicts, the differences, and we wind up focusing our attention on negativity. We look at what we're trying to accomplish and all we see is how much is left instead of how far we've already come.

It's easy to get caught up in thinking about what's missing and what hasn't happened yet. We did that for a long time with Walter. There were constant reminders about what "should" be happening for him and with him, and that just wasn't our reality. It was unfair to focus on what was lacking, and if we'd continued down that path, we would have unfairly limited his progress.

When Walter laughs, and I mean really laughs, it's a full-body, deep-from-his-belly laugh. It's impossible not to at least smile when he's doing it. I challenge anyone not to laugh along with him, even if you don't know what he finds so funny. When his face lights up, and his attention is hooked by a new song or a favorite cartoon, it's pure magic. He surprises himself. His smile in those moments is absolute pride and confidence. There's nothing like watching him strut into his classroom and high five his teachers.

We could have missed all that. We could have allowed ourselves to stay in the place where his difference was a series of limitations. We still have those. He can't play as long as some of his peers, he's easily overwhelmed by crowds and noise, and he needs to stop regularly throughout the day to eat through his feeding tube. Those details are part of our family life, and we've gotten great at working with them and making sure that Walter has the accommodations he needs while Oscar and Arthur still have opportunities to do what they want to do and be more involved with their friends.

One of my favorite things is to watch the three of them interact and play. Sometimes, there's a struggle over a toy, but more often than not, one of the younger boys will say, "Walter, take a turn," or "Walter, here's the book you like." Their bond is one that continues to grow, and I truly believe that Oscar and Arthur will be kinder, more patient adults when they grow up. We celebrate that with them every chance we get. "You guys are such good brothers," or "I love how thoughtful you are," or "Thanks for making sure everyone is included" are said almost daily in our kitchen.

The effect it has on their confidence is immediately visible. Shoulders push back, they stand a little taller, and they smile big smiles. I want them to always take the time to recognize when things are going well. That way, when things aren't going well, they have something they can pull from or look back to. Whatever the circumstances are, good or bad, they're temporary. Nothing will be completely wonderful or completely awful all of the time. We need a bit of both. The memory of the high can make the low more bearable, and the lows help us lean into celebrating the highs.

Creating Inch Stones for the Whole Family

We also use inch stones with our neuro-typical boys. We're just starting them at 5 and 6 years old with the idea of weekly chores and an allowance. Oscar wants to buy a fish, but he wants to earn all the money on his own. Arthur doesn't have anything specific he wants to buy, but he doesn't want to be left out. We're going to start with one or two things they'll be responsible for each day or each week, and then as they get consistent and confident with those tasks, we'll add more. I'm particularly excited to pass the baton for doing the dinner dishes.

One area where we've seen this concept illustrated for them is in their Tae Kwon Do classes. The way their teacher structures the program, they focus on one skill at a time—punching, kicking, form, or learning to speak Korean. Each time they master one area for their current belt level, they get a different color of tape around the end of their belts. They can see how much progress they're making, they know what to focus on next, and they get so excited for each accomplishment. They know exactly what comes next, and that momentum carries them between their weekly classes.

In our house, trying something new is always worth celebrating. Whether it's tasting a new food or trying a different activity, the effort is what matters. Didn't like the food? No problem—you know that now because you tried. And who knows? Maybe next time, your tastes will surprise you. Arthur is learning how to read, and he gets words wrong. We sound them out, we practice, and the next time he reads that book, he gets more words right.

I talk to them about being excited to learn and wanting to learn things together. It's a message I need to hear too. The first step is a big deal in our house. That willingness to learn and be a beginner is something that I see in my work in human resources all the time. I can teach a program or a process, but the interest in learning, the willingness to take feedback are often much harder to teach adults. Looking for and listening to feedback is one of the most important things you can do to track your progress and see how far you've really come.

Reflecting on Progress: Look Back with Gratitude

Looking back at your progress, especially when it feels like things are taking longer than you'd like, requires shifting your mindset to focus on growth rather than just outcomes. It's easy to get frustrated when the destination still feels far away, but reflection is about recognizing how far you've already come and appreciating the small wins along the way. Progress is rarely a straight line—it often involves setbacks, detours, and adjustments, all of which are valuable experiences that contribute to your growth. It's easy to get caught up in looking forward and seeing what's left and forgetting about all you've already done. That's another way that celebrating the inch stones can help along the way.

When reflecting, it helps to zoom out and look at the bigger picture. Even if you're not exactly where you want to be, ask yourself: What have you learned? What obstacles have you overcome? Which skills, habits, or insights have you developed that you didn't have at the start? These questions highlight the often-invisible progress that's been happening beneath the surface. It's also useful to revisit your initial goals and compare them to where you are now—you might find that even slow progress has brought you much closer than you realize.

Tracking small milestones along the way can also provide concrete reminders of your achievements. Journals, to-do lists, or even looking at old notes or checklists can show that meaningful steps have been made, even if they didn't feel significant in the moment. Celebrating these small victories helps build momentum and keeps motivation alive.

Lastly, remember that timing is part of the process. Some goals take longer because they require deeper growth, more learning, or external factors beyond your control. Trust that progress, no matter how slow, is still movement in the right direction. Every step forward—even the smallest one—matters, and looking back with kindness and gratitude can reignite your belief in yourself and the journey ahead.

You don't have to wait for the perfect moment to start or celebrate. Just like Walter's small steps added up to something wonderful, your small actions—whether in work, personal growth, or family life—are worth celebrating right now.

Your Plan for Celebrating Inch Stones

So here's what you need to do so that your celebrations throughout the year get you to a place where you feel so proud and accomplished by December 31st.

1. Pick your goal.
2. Make your plan and map out the milestones and the inch stones.
3. Pick which inch stones you'll use as your points for celebration.
4. Decide how to track and celebrate your progress.
5. Take the very first step.

Progress isn't about how fast you go or how perfect each step is—it's about staying on the path, no matter how winding it becomes. So, what small step will you celebrate today?

Chapter 3

Looking Within to Move Forward in Peace: Silencing the Inner Critic

By Rebecca McCartney, LCSW

"IF SOMETHING IN YOU YOURSELF SAYS 'YOU AREN'T A PAINTER'—IT'S THEN THAT YOU SHOULD PAINT...AND THAT VOICE WILL BE SILENCED..." –VINCENT VAN GOGH[9]

I've always been a reader. As a child, I would lie awake at night reading until I could no longer keep my eyes open. I enjoyed series like *Nancy Drew* and *The Boxcar Children*. I loved anything written by Beverly Cleary and could spend hours in my pre-teen years flipping through dozens of volumes of Jane Magazine. My favorite book that I read on repeat was the 1968 Newbery Medal winner *From the Mixed-up Files of Mrs. Basil E. Frankweiler* by E.L. Konigsburg.[10] I still re-read it every few years and continue to find joy in the adventures of Claudia Kincaid and her brother

---

[9] Van Gogh, Vincent. "To Theo van Gogh." Sunday, 28 October 1883. Letter #400. Van Gogh Museum Amsterdam. https://www.vangoghmuseum.nl/en/highlights/letters/400. November 10, 2024.

[10] Konigsburg, E.L. *From the Mixed-up Files of Mrs. Basil E. Frankweiler*. Atheneum Publishers, 1967.

Jamie as they explore the Metropolitan Museum of Art. As much as I loved reading, I think more specifically, I've always loved words. My favorite subjects in school were English, spelling and anything language arts-related. As an adolescent, I indiscriminately collected quotes I loved. My bubble cursive handwriting preserved wisdom, whether from Nietzsche, Ayn Rand, Oprah, or Voltaire. I was an equal opportunity quote collector, relishing the inspiration I found there. I organized them in a one-inch binder filled with notebook paper. I also read entirely too much scripture as a child and teenager. More than was probably developmentally appropriate. I'm not sure if it was because of my upbringing (Preacher's Kid here) or because I simply found it genuinely beautiful. I still do.

Because of my love of words and reading, I also began to develop a love for writing. I kept notebooks full of bad poetry and partially written short stories. I occasionally wrote to process my thoughts and feelings when I needed to make sense of them, but I desperately wanted to be someone who journaled regularly. The idea of daily chronicling life's ups and downs and having those stories preserved to reflect back on later seemed like a dream. I made attempts at regular journaling throughout my childhood, adolescence and even into adulthood. My good intention displayed itself in that each December, I would faithfully buy a beautiful new journal; its clean, crisp pages brimming with possibility. Then on January 1st, I would dutifully begin writing in my new journal, embarking on my new practice that I was sure would spark creativity, as well as personal and spiritual growth throughout the new year. And every year, I would commit myself to this daily endeavor 100%! Until approximately January 3rd. I wanted to journal. I planned to journal. I had a deep desire to journal. Alas, I could not journal. My bookcase became a veritable graveyard where the tainted journals were laid to rest, a constant reminder of my failure.

Often at the beginning of a new year, I look at what I wish were different. I imagine the best of me: my body, my spiritual life, my relationships, my career, or my home. Maybe I want to eat healthier, learn a new hobby, or develop better communication in my closest relationships. Perhaps I want to take on a new project at work, declutter my house, or be more consistent in my prayer life. I'm hopeful for change, but often from the very outset, I either struggle to start, or once I've begun, I struggle to keep moving. Can you relate? Do you know the areas you want to change, but either can't start or have trouble keeping momentum once you've begun? As you face a brand-new year, my hope is that you would learn why this happens, what you can do about it, and ultimately feel confident and competent to accomplish your goals.

To better understand why you often feel stuck, it's helpful to learn a bit about one of the most well-known and most effective therapeutic techniques available to therapists like me, Cognitive Behavioral Therapy (CBT). CBT helps a person better understand how their thoughts, feelings and actions are connected. Often, CBT focuses on helping people change negative self-talk. Negative self-talk is the automatic, self-critical, repetitive thoughts that influence a person's feelings. It often begins without warning, usually in reaction to a trigger. The start of a new year, for many, has the potential to trigger negative self-talk.

Negative self-talk is a tactic of what cognitive behavioral therapists call the inner critic. Your inner critic is the voice in your head that analyzes, criticizes, and belittles. It causes you to question yourself, convincing you that you're worthless and incapable. It zaps your self-confidence and instills self-doubt. Your inner critic has declared herself the presiding judge over every word you speak and every action you take. It is your inner critic who is using negative self-talk to derail you from the changes you want to make this new year.

In order to learn to recognize your own negative self-talk, it's helpful to define seven common types. These examples aren't specific to the negative self-talk often encountered in a new year, but rather drawn from my therapy practice over the years.

All-or-nothing thinking—this type of negative self-talk operates in extremes or absolutes. It's often called black and white thinking because it cannot consider the factors that exist in the gray. (Ex. My child will either grow up to be a huge success or a total failure.)

Should-ing—focuses on the belief that there's always more a person "should" be doing. It creates a lack of self-confidence by assuming one is operating below their best effort, is somehow obligated to act, and is never quite doing enough. (Ex. I should go to an event even when I don't want to because it's expected that I'll be there.)

Catastrophizing—causes people to fear or assume the worst about a situation, even when they lack the necessary information to make that conclusion. (Ex. What if my son was in a car accident, and that's why he's not answering his phone?)

Overgeneralization—a person believes one experience applies to every other similar situation. (Ex. My boyfriend broke up with me, so obviously I'm bad at relationships.)

Emotional Reasoning—a person believes something simply because it feels true. This type of thinking bases actions *only* on feelings and considers feelings absolute truth. (Ex. If I feel anxious after I make a decision, therefore it must mean I made the wrong decision.)

Personalization—assuming an action is related to you personally whether it was intended for you/connected to you or not. (Ex. I didn't receive an invitation to an event, which means the host must not like me.)

Jumping to Conclusions—when a person makes negative predictions about the future. (Ex. I see a mole on my arm and assume it's cancerous before going to the dermatologist to get it checked out.)

Becoming familiar with some of the types of negative self-talk will serve to help you get unstuck and back to working on your goals. Remember my journaling issue I mentioned earlier? I set a goal, developed a plan to execute, and even made it to the starting part. But before I could gain much momentum, I stalled out. My negative self-talk immobilized me and sounded something like this: "Because you missed a day, your journal is ruined (catastrophizing). This is what you always do, Rebecca. You never follow through on commitments or accomplish the goals you set (all-or-nothing thinking). You should be able to do something as simple as writing five minutes a day (should-ing). It's not even worth trying again, because clearly you're never going to be a person who journals every day (overgeneralizing)." She's a real jerk, my inner critic. Let me introduce you.

I call her Negative Nellie. She was first given this name by my mom when I was a child. Anytime I was being especially pessimistic, my mom would remind me, "It's okay to notice the downside of things, but constantly focusing your attention on the negative does nothing but make you and everyone around you miserable. Nobody likes a Negative Nellie." As I grew up, I continued to call my inner critic Negative Nellie not only because of my mom, but also because she reminded me of Nellie Olesen from the old TV show *Little House on the Prairie*.[11] Remember her? She was the brat with the bouncy, blonde curls. Her annoying know-it-all attitude combined with her signature whiny voice made her the girl none of the other kids wanted to be around. You may have a name for your inner critic, too. If not, I suggest naming her. Personifying this voice helps defuse self-criticism by providing separation from your own identity, but also, it's just more fun.

So how is it that we each have an inner critic? Where did she come from? It's generally understood that the inner critic is developed in childhood by listening and observing your parents or other important adults in your life. You internalized hurtful words or unhealthy behavior, and they became the only measure of whether you were competent and capable. Many of you received affirming messages in your developmental years that encouraged you and made you believe you could do anything you wanted to do. This wasn't espe-

---
[11] Hanalis, Blanche. *Little House on the Prairie*. NBC Productions, 1974. *Amazon Prime*, https://www.amazon.com/Little-House-Prairie-Season-1/dp/B00J8BYAUI.

cially helpful because it wasn't entirely true. You can't actually do everything you want to do. There are some things that you won't be able to accomplish simply because you don't have the ability, experience or needed skill set. Some of you received negative messages that said you weren't enough, and you'd always fall short. This was also untrue. You actually don't fail at every turn like you were conditioned to believe. You have successes and failures like all humans. Still others of you received a combination of affirming and negative messages, often shared simultaneously. These left you feeling confused about your value or abilities. Not surprisingly, the negative messages were often the ones you believed and helped shape your sense of worth.

As you grew, the negative messages and feelings of uncertainty about your worth were fueled by comparison. Beginning incredibly early, you probably began to compare yourself to others. You noticed how your body shape or size, hair, or skin compared to others. You compared your grades, your friends, and your clothes. Most of you, like me, found that your tendency toward comparison really amped up in the pre-teen years. At a time when you felt the most awkward and ugly, it sure felt like you weren't good enough. Comparison to others slowly solidified your self-doubt. You got distracted by your own perceived weaknesses, and then focused on the progress of the others around you. Comparison tricked you into believing that someone else's success was the ruler by which you should measure your own.

The inner critic, complete with her negative self-talk, clearly needs to be managed. You have several options in how you choose to deal with your inner critic. You could ignore her. Try not to listen, and hope the negative self-talk goes away. Some therapists do believe there are times when this is preferable, but for most people in the majority of circumstances, this method is not effective. Distracting for a bit may provide some relief, but eventually, usually fairly quickly, the thoughts come back. Typically, your inner critic won't be ignored and is too smart to be distracted. You could shame her. Try to turn her tactics against her and make her feel bad about how she's treating you. At this point in your life, I'm guessing you've figured out that all shame does is make you feel worse. It's not a great catalyst for change. Another option is to coddle your inner critic, making excuses for her in the name of self-compassion. Unfortunately, this usually leads to a stronger belief in the critic's message rather than a healthy reassessment. It doesn't seem to me that ignoring, shaming, or coddling will do the trick. I'd like to suggest another option. If you want to be able to set goals and maintain momentum this year, you need to get your inner critic to shut up, or at least learn to use her inside voice. Get curious about your inner critic, seek to understand her, and convince her to change the way she speaks to you. This is quite a feat because your inner critic is condescending, critical, self-defeating, and often only sees in black and white. She is pessimistic, points out all the ways you aren't good enough, and frankly, can be a bully. She relies on her excellent memory to quickly remind you of your past failures, dumb decisions and missed marks. And while her destructive behavior can exert control over you if you allow, you can turn the tables. You see, along with her excellent memory, she is also a quick study. She can be trained to think differently, to focus more attention on the positive, and to encourage rather than tear down. You can transform her voice from one who critiques you to the voice who notices possibility.

CBT offers many tools to help you silence your inner critic by looking within. I'd like to focus on three. The first tool is called cognitive reframing. Reframing allows you to change negative self-talk into something more realistic and accurate. It focuses less on the negative and helps you recognize that your problems or thoughts can be viewed in multiple ways. It teaches you to ask yourself questions like, "Is there a different way I could think about this?" or "Could I be missing some important information?" It's important that the reframe is believable. It can't be overly positive to the point that it feels impossible or untrue. Let's practice with a few examples of negative self-talk we may encounter as we think about possible goals for the new year. Notice the type of negative self-talk, as well as the suggestion to reframe.

	Negative Self-Talk	Cognitive Reframe
should-ing	I should try to lose some weight this year. I'm not happy with my appearance and I should make more of an effort to be healthier.	I would like to be healthier and feel more confident in my body. I could choose to lose weight, but I could also choose to focus on my overall health this year. It's my choice.
overgeneralizing	I've been a messy person my whole life. I keep too much and don't throw things away. I don't have it in me to keep a clean house free of clutter. I might as well accept this is who I really am.	It's true I've never been the tidiest person. It's also true that I've not really attempted to change this about myself before now. I'm ready to live differently.
emotional reasoning	I feel like the worst mom ever. I'm inconsistent and short-tempered with my kids. I feel like a total failure. I'm sure my children will suffer because of my inadequate parenting.	Feeling like a failure is different than being a failure. My feelings don't always tell me the truth. I've had failures as a parent, but I've also had moments for which I'm extremely proud. My kids see both.

Cognitive reframing can be especially challenging if you've been speaking to yourself in a negative way for a long time. As you're learning to reframe negative self-talk, it can be helpful to imagine you are reframing for a friend or another adult. It's often easier to take a different perspective when it doesn't relate to you personally. Keep trying. It will become easier the more you practice. I'd like to share an example, again from my therapy practice, of how reframing negative thoughts can have a big impact.

Crystal came to me initially struggling with symptoms related to depression. She found it difficult to get up and shower, go to work or take care of her children. As I began to listen to Crystal and get to know her, I learned just how loudly her inner critic spoke. Due to trauma in her childhood, she had developed a pretty consistent stream of negative self-talk that caused a deeply held belief that she was stupid, incompetent, and generally worthless. I taught her about the inner critic and trauma's effects. I explained the tool of reframing and how it works. Crystal had a hard time using this tool because every reframe she came up with felt like a lie and she just couldn't get behind it. She felt silly and it wasn't helping. During one session when she became frustrated with the process, I asked Crystal to pretend that I was the client, and she was the therapist. We even switched seats. I shared a moment of negative self-talk I'd experienced earlier that week—*You're not a good therapist. You don't have any business helping other people when you struggle with your own anxiety.* I encouraged her to help me reframe that thought—*Your own anxiety doesn't define whether the therapy you provide is effective.* Then we switched back. I asked her what it was like for her, and she began to cry. Crystal explained that it made her so sad knowing I would think those things about myself. I told her it also made me sad to hear the negative, hurtful things she was believing about herself. I might have teared up at this point, too. We tried reframing again using another of her negative thoughts, and this time, fairly quickly, she was able to suggest a more positive reframe that felt believable. We processed this together and she realized that the breakthrough happened when the thought didn't relate to her personally. She was able to see how hurtful and painful those negative beliefs can be when she was seeing them from my perspective. In the weeks that followed, Crystal began to dismantle her negative beliefs one by one. I hate to spoil the ending, but guess who no longer experiences regular symptoms of depression?

The second tool you can use on your inner critic is called Socratic questioning. Socratic questioning challenges negative thoughts by asking a series of questions to help you get closer and closer to the truth. These questions force you to examine your thoughts objectively. This tool can be extremely helpful because thoughts come and go so quickly, you must be intentional about slowing down long enough to question them and challenge the conclusions you've reached. I'll first illustrate how this tool works using a negative thought related to my earlier journaling example.

A Peaceful New Year

Thought to be questioned:
You should be able to do something as simple as writing five minutes a day.

> What is the evidence for this thought? Against it?

> Am I basing this thought on facts or on feelings?

> Is this thought black and white when in reality it's more complicated?

> Am I having this thought out of habit?

> Might someone else have a different interpretation of this same situation?

When I work through these questions and allow myself to analyze the thought, I realize pretty quickly how many types of negative self-talk are showing up. I'm also able to see my poor reasoning. Working through the Socratic questions helped me to see that I was basing my thought on feeling ashamed because I couldn't do what felt like a simple task. I realized I didn't have any facts to support the idea that I "should" be able to write daily. The questions also helped me to look at my thought from a different perspective. I realized that someone else might tell me that I'm in a busy season of my life, and they understand why it would be difficult to commit to writing daily.

Willa's story is an example from my work with a former client of how using Socratic questioning can reduce anxious thoughts, specifically worry about the future. Willa came in for therapy because she wasn't sleeping. She was stuck in a loop of worrisome thoughts that were plaguing her all day and then wouldn't shut off when she wanted to go to sleep at night. She was exhausted, irritable, unable to focus on her job, and wanted to try therapy before asking for a sleep aid from her doctor. I asked Willa to tell me more about her anxious thoughts and we determined they fell into three specific categories: the past, the present, and the future. Great. She was literally worrying about everything—past regrets, present stressors, and future possibilities. I thought we'd start with future worries, and that perhaps Socratic questioning could be a good tool to try. We identified one very specific recurring negative thought (a future worry), and we worked through the following questions.

> **Willa's worry to be questioned:**
> What if I get cancer, have to do treatment, and then die and leave my children without a mother?

> What are some clues that your worry will not come true?

> If your worries do not come true, what could happen instead?

> If your worries do come true, how would you handle it? Do you believe you would eventually be ok?

As we worked through the questions, Willa was able to see her worry more objectively. She was able to see a lack of evidence that she is likely to get sick: she sees her doctor regularly for check-ups, has no history of cancer in her family, and takes good care of her body through a healthy diet and regular exercise. Because of the different elements of her negative thoughts, we were able to talk about the many realistic possibilities. For example, it's possible she would never get cancer, or it's possible she would get cancer, need treatment, and then go into remission. Willa was able to express her fears that the worry in its entirety would come true and then processed how she imagined she would handle it. She recognized that ultimately, she was afraid of having to leave her children and described how incredibly sad that made her. We were able to isolate that thought and work back through the questions. At the conclusion of the questions, I asked her how her worry had changed, and she shared that although she still felt some worry, she realized how unlikely it was that it would come true. She also said that she believed that if that time ever came, she knew she would have the strength from God and support from family and friends to face whatever came. We were able to isolate many more future worries of Willa's and drastically reduce the thoughts. We then moved to the present stressors she was worrying about and used Socratic questioning similar to the questions from my journaling example. She was able to identify the specific types of negative self-talk that were getting her stuck and learned to see her current circumstances from a different perspective. As those thoughts began to reduce significantly, we homed in on her past regret. These we tackled with a combination of learning to practice self-forgiveness, making amends to those she could, and additional work around unprocessed trauma that was showing up.

The third tool from CBT that is helpful when working to silence your inner critic is called behavioral activation, and it works differently than the first two tools. In both cognitive reframing and Socratic questioning, the goal is to first change your thoughts in order to affect feelings and behavior. But with behavioral activation, you work backwards, beginning with a change in behavior first, and then allowing that behavior change to create more positive feelings which lead to more positive thoughts. Behavioral activation can be helpful when you are struggling with motivation or uncertainty about how to begin. By having a specific activity to do with a starting point and end point, it feels more manageable.

Behavioral activation helps silence your inner critic by reducing self-doubt, rebuilding self-trust, and increasing self-confidence. Your past behavior has often given you evidence that you don't follow through and complete goals. You said you would do something and then you didn't. Breaking this promise to yourself created a lack of self-trust. When you've let yourself down and proven you can't be trusted, you have to create new evidence to suggest you're the kind of person who follows through on the promises you make to yourself. One way to start rebuilding self-trust using behavioral activation is to begin keeping regular small promises to yourself daily. This can be especially helpful in the new year because of the difficulty we often have maintaining momentum. Behavioral activation works because as you create consistent trustworthy behavior, not only will positive thoughts and feelings follow, but your self-confidence will begin to overtake your self-doubt! Your inner critic will be silenced as she has no choice but to be inundated with thoughts of the times you were successful, not only the times when you failed.

With each passing day, keeping these small promises create seeds of self-trust that begin to replace self-doubt. In the same way other people in your life earn your trust by keeping their promises to you, you can also learn to trust yourself by your consistent, trustworthy behavior. Let's use an earlier example of negative self-talk to illustrate how behavioral activation works. It can accomplish a similar goal of positive feelings and positive thoughts, but by beginning with behavior change.

I decided to use this behavioral activation tool and see if it could help me work through my negative self-talk related to journaling. I picked a behavior I could commit to and was able to change my self-talk.

Although I proved to myself I was capable of becoming a person who journals daily, I realized something that surprised me. I wanted to make a different choice. I chose to buy pretty journals I love with no guilt. I gave myself permission to spend $7.99 per journal at TJ Maxx, deciding I could indeed afford this habit. I chose to enjoy these journals by using them to make to-do lists, jot client notes during session, or craft blog posts to be typed later. I decided that what actually matters to me is being a person who practices writing and becomes better. So, I'm writing. When and where I can. But now I know, if I wanted to be someone who journals daily, I *totally* could.

At the beginning of a new year, your inner critic can get really loud. She senses the possibility of failure, and she knows you're vulnerable. Her familiar negative self-talk, self-doubt, distrust, and general bad attitude all begin with a whisper, and then bombard your confidence. You see your neat and tidy list of New Year's Resolutions, your goals and objectives written out in pretty colored pens, and then she reminds you of all the failed attempts and the unkept promises. You then start to believe you can't be trusted. When that happens, I hope you remember that although there could be some hint of truth to what your inner critic is saying, it's never the whole truth. Using the tools of cognitive reframing, Socratic questioning, and behavioral activation, your inner critic can be taught how to change unhelpful negative thoughts, question unhealthy beliefs, and behave in trustworthy ways.

Learning to silence your inner critic will be a lifelong pursuit. There will always be more personal improvement goals or intentions to achieve greater spiritual health. As long as you're alive, you'll want to continue growing, changing, and improving. My encouragement to you this new year, your quiet new year, is that you pull out that long list of New Year's Resolutions you made, mark through everything except the one or two things that matter the most to you. Start small and commit. Instead of feeling ashamed that you didn't accomplish all your resolutions, you'll be proud of the changes you made, and will be ready to tackle a few more goals next year. I believe in you.

A Prayer for Your New Year

"Lord, as I enter this new year, I pray that I grow in my understanding of the connections between my thoughts, feelings, and behaviors. I pray for emotional maturity that helps me in my relationships with You and others. I ask You to open my mind to accepting opportunities to change my negative thoughts that are keeping me stuck, sad and discontent. I pray I will learn to listen to my needs and respond to them consistently, never feeling selfish or ashamed, but grateful and wise. I pray, always trusting in your help and guidance, that I will begin to keep small promises to myself, allowing confidence to grow and self-doubt to shrink. In Jesus name, Amen."

Chapter 4

Shedding the Old Way: Clothing Yourself with Christ in the New Year

By Jennifer Gorham, Psy.D.

> THEREFORE, AS GOD'S CHOSEN PEOPLE, HOLY AND DEARLY LOVED, CLOTHE YOURSELVES WITH COMPASSION, KINDNESS, HUMILITY, GENTLENESS, AND PATIENCE.
> —COLOSSIANS 3:12

"How do I do this? I should know how to do this."

My mother and I stand in the bathroom. She has a broken arm, ulcer wound, and wrinkled body; I have a washcloth and no knowledge of how to give a sponge bath. Earlier that morning, I almost googled how to give a sponge bath but hesitated, fearing what visuals that search might bring. Tentatively, as Mom watches, I fill the sink with warm water and soap, focusing on what I do know because I am completely out of my element. In the last three months, Mom has fallen twice, resulting in hospital and rehab stays and multiple injuries. These months have been chock full of new responsibilities, unanswered questions, uncertainty, lots of unsolicited opinions, and anxiety. I've faced all of them (not so sure how well, but definitely faced them), and yet, here in the bathroom, I feel small and unprepared.

Mom offers guidance since she has had so many sponge baths in the hospital and rehab. I feel myself detaching, shutting down my emotions to focus on the task. It is uncomfortable being close to my mother's aging and wounded body, and my own inadequacy blares at me like a foghorn of shame.

The last year has been a new and challenging one for Mom and me. My dad died a few years ago, and Mom moved away from her home of 38 years to be near my family. It's the first year we have lived near each other for 28 of those. Conflict between us has made it sometimes challenging to feel compassion toward her. Historically, the distance made this easier to manage, but here we are, only inches away from each other rather than states and miles. Shutting down my emotions is often how I cope when close in proximity; it theoretically keeps me from unintentionally lashing out in anger and frustration.

But this morning is different. I stay present, not of my own striving but through the gentle nudge of the Holy Spirit. I make eye contact, look at my mom, and begin to wash her body gently and gingerly. After only a few seconds, an overwhelming infusion of compassion for her floods me, and tears spring to my eyes. My heart softens, and my hands become gentler.

This is not my typical experience when confronted with pain or wounds. Most of my life, I have experienced conflict between focusing on a task or a person. I feel successful and efficient when completing a to-do list. Connections and emotion, or just plain old interactions with people, slow down this success and efficiency. I am, it turns out, an incredibly impatient person, not inherently gentle, even when my heart is to see people and processes reach their full potential or completion. Even when flooded with compassion in that bathroom, I was so overwhelmed I tried to shut down these tender emotions because I needed to get the task done. The intense vulnerability in such a small space left me grasping for a sense of control. Gentleness and unrestrained drivenness cannot coexist.

Unrestrained drivenness is often what defines our thoughts about the new year. Resolutions and goals are rooted in our desire to be better, something other than what we currently are. Our intentions disintegrate quickly in the face of real life, often because they are unreasonable and unattainable. Thoughts of what we want to change are often driven by what society tells us is important—nutrition, sleep, exercise, achievement. God offers another intention to us as we begin a new year.

An Unexpected Invitation

Paul says in Colossians 3:12 to clothe ourselves with gentleness and a host of other virtues that are easy to list and hard to embody, both with those we love and those who challenge us. The Greek word translated "clothe" indicates a sinking into, like the sinking of the setting sun into the horizon. Consider what it is like to wear a new or borrowed piece of clothing. You are aware of all the places it doesn't fit; your skin is more alive to the fabric, even if you like the feel of it. It must be worn many times before it becomes something you sink into, as I do the most comfortable sweats I have had since college. These become like a second skin, and we reach for them when we have a hard day or just need to breathe and relax. While we wear these comfortable clothes occasionally, Paul says we are to clothe ourselves with gentleness and the virtues as a second skin all the time.

Imagine this New Year's practice: As you dress in the morning and choose your shirt, you intentionally choose gentleness. As you pull on your pants or skirt, you pull on compassion. Socks invite patience and shoes humility. Kindness is chosen along with putting on our hat or glasses. This is quite the idyllic scene! To be honest, though, these attributes don't seem like they will get us far in today's world. We might get hurt, taken advantage of, walked over, or overlooked. The world tells us to pull on strength, confidence, guardedness, and assertiveness. These line up well with culture's ideas of goals and resolutions. I know which one I naturally gravitate toward, and it's not Paul's fashion sense. Is there a way I can be both—strong and gentle?

This would be a good moment to define gentleness. Gentleness is described in Greek as power under control. My favorite example of this is holding a newborn. Babies have no control over their bodies and depend on someone else's arms for structure and safety. I'm incredibly aware of my strength and responsibility when I hold a baby, that I need to hold with gentleness and strength. Too tightly squashes, too loosely risks a fall or loss of head control. Gentleness is a constant understanding of how much structure and space are required and flexing between these needs. Gentleness is not laying down power and strength but channeling them rightly for the sake of the other.

Shedding the Old Way

Prior to telling the Colossians to clothe themselves with these virtues, Paul tells them to take off their old selves, the clothes of sexual immorality, impurity, evil desires, greed, anger, rage, malice, slander, lying, and filthy language. He notes that the new clothes cannot go on over these old clothes. These clothes are often worn as armor, as they feel stronger and more protective of our most tender longings and desires. Greed covers inadequacy, anger covers hurt and humiliation, sexual impurity can cover abuse or a longing to be seen and valued, and lying covers our fear of accountability or being seen as dumb. Each covering demonstrates our own striving to heal our wounds and protect from further pain. This armor Paul says we must shed before we put on the new clothes for the new self that is "being renewed in knowledge in the image of its Creator." Paul does not tell them to clothe themselves with their new virtues until they need protection. Paul says to stay in these virtuous clothes until they become a second skin. In fact, he goes on in verse 13 that **with these clothes on**, they are to bear with each other and forgive one another as the Lord forgives. This is a risky relationship where we remain exposed in a posture of vulnerability as we walk with Jesus. Our new self reflects the image and character of Father, Jesus, and Holy Spirit, who authored creation and whom we would never describe as weak. He is gentle *and* strong.

What Gets in the Way

After 20 years as a psychologist and four decades of living, I know that I am not alone in my trouble with gentleness. People defend against gentleness and compassion, as this might lead to repeated pain, and they often come to therapy for support in processing humiliation, shame, rejection, disappointment, abandonment, and betrayal. Relational hurts and life pain often result in trying to protect ourselves in a myriad of creative ways. The desire to flee from or fight pain is protective and normal, and sometimes necessary.

When I cut my finger a few years ago, I protected it with a bandage and careful movement for a few weeks, which was necessary for short-term healing. Wounds are weak and make us vulnerable, so they require a harder shell for a little while. The challenges are choosing appropriate protection and taking it off when it is time.

If I chose to leave the wound open or cover it with a towel, infection would be more likely. If I continued to protect the wound long after it healed, my world would shrink over time. I would shower differently, I would avoid certain tools in the kitchen, I would maybe begin to avoid recipes that require that food that I had to cut, and I would avoid typing on my computer, which would affect my work. The same is true in emotional pain. When we chronically protect ourselves unnecessarily, we create barriers to intimacy and healthy relationships. When I keep myself from being known through anger, avoidance, people-pleasing, or hurtful words of my own, I inadvertently close myself off to others, effectively hardening my heart. This does not heal hurts and wounds but leaves them open to infection, re-wounding us even while we try to protect ourselves. We are not able to be truly known or to know others, leaving us lonely and disconnected. Shallow connection results from avoiding honesty and openness to serve our fear of rejection, harshness, or worse, abandonment.

Loneliness is so rampant today that the UK instituted a Loneliness Minister in 2021 to address the emotional epidemic.[12] A physician friend here in the US has said for years, long before the COVID pandemic, that he wished he could prescribe friends and community for his patients, seeing so many who come in just to have someone to talk to. If you feel lonely, you are not alone. If you are around people often and still feel lonely, you are not alone. Disconnection happens sometimes due to work and life demands, but people retreat from deep relationships daily for other reasons. Here are a few:

- not sharing your perspective to avoid conflict
- avoiding someone you are annoyed with rather than hurt their feelings by saying something
- avoiding telling your spouse how you feel because you fear being dismissed
- talking intellectually about something you feel deeply emotional about over-thinking how to respond to someone
- not sharing for fear of sounding stupid to others
- avoiding sharing the depth of your anxiety and depression because you want to be seen as "having it all together"

---

[12] Walker, Peter. "May Appoints Minister to Tackle Loneliness Issues Raised by Jo Cox." *The Guardian*, 16 Jan. 2018, www.theguardian.com/society/2018/jan/16/may-appoints-minister-tackle-loneliness-issues-raised-jo-cox. Accessed 8 Feb. 2018.

- deflecting with humor when you could share vulnerably
- not saying the reason you are afraid
- not supporting a friend through something hard because you fear saying or doing the 'wrong' thing
- withholding relationship due to anger or frustration
- nursing contempt, disappointment, or anger so as not to be hurt again
- turning to the phone instead of connecting with someone
- not apologizing when you know you need to

Shame and fear keep us isolated. Isolation can make us hard-hearted.

What do we do then? Can we be gentle and compassionate, humble and kind with others without being vulnerable? The answer is NO. It is possible to look gentle and do the right compassionate thing without being driven by genuine, compassionate feelings. Shallow gentleness results from our own striving to be what we think others want us to be, who we believe we should be, or who God wants us to be. Shallow gentleness avoids hurting other people's feelings by not saying things that need addressing relationally but also drives a wall between two people. Shallow gentleness peters out when others don't respond the way we want or feel they should in response to our kind actions. Gentleness requires a relaxed posture, where we aren't tied to outcomes. When outcomes aren't what we want or expect, we find out if our gentleness is substantive. Paul's virtues are not costumes to put on for a performance, but the clothes that we sink into that become who we are.

An Unexpected Path Toward Gentleness

It is clear in the New Testament that God desires us to clothe ourselves with these virtues, as this language is used in multiple letters from multiple authors. But we also want God's protection from hurt and disappointment and the shame felt when rejected, misunderstood, or misperceived. I confess that these clothes He wants us to wear feel flimsy and sheer. Thankfully, we can turn to Ephesians 6, where Paul writes about God's offered armor, the full armor of God. Paul begins Ephesians re-rooting the church in the good news of Jesus reconciling us to Himself, the Father, and the Spirit. The gospel that Paul shares is that we are loved beyond measure, seen for all of who we are, and invited into the gentle perfection of Jesus to be the covering for our imperfect humanity. Paul then addresses relational issues in the Ephesian church, between members of the faith community, husbands and wives, household masters and slaves. He notes the reality that **how we interact with each other** has an impact on the community at large. Paul moves from talking about how we in Christ's church interact with one another to how we stand in the face of evil. He is not talking about how we debate or defend the gospel here; Paul says, "Put on the full armor of God, so that you can take your stand against the devil's schemes" (verse 11). The enemy's primary schemes involve breaking down relationships of love and authenticity within the body of Christ and breaking down our relationship of love, identity, and authenticity with Jesus Himself.

The armor of God addresses these weak points. The armor is unified in its protection of our standing before God and relationship with Him. Paul is not distinguishing each piece of armor as its own unique protection but offers an image of a fully protected body with the reality of our identity in Christ. We are His, His chosen people, holy and dearly loved. Each part of armor reminds us of this truth. The belt of truth cinches us with the truth of our identity in Jesus through the gospel. We can stand, not in our own strength and willpower, but in Jesus' blood covering us, the breastplate of righteousness. The gospel of peace, the helmet of salvation, and the sword of the Spirit are all different ways of saying that we are fully protected by Jesus' love and righteousness as His children, wholly and dearly loved. This whole-body armor absorbs the pain when we hurt. When Jesus takes the full impact of the blow, we rest in His love and healing, and from knowledge of His love and security, we can respond gently and honestly to others. Our need for approval, belonging, security, and control fade in comparison to the security we find with Jesus.

From the beginning in the garden, the enemy primarily attacked God's character and our humanity and identity. The armor of God protects who God is and who we are. We will experience rejection, hurt, and difficulty, but we are protected as Jesus absorbs these so that we can sink into His gentleness and let these overflow to others around us. With the story at the beginning, I let Jesus absorb the shame of my inadequacy and pain from wounds with my mom. Even for a few moments, gentleness flowed out. The protection of this armor allows us to continue in gentleness and associated virtues. We don't have to worry about taking them off or reaching for our old armor; we don't have to worry about feeling vulnerable because we are protected by the most amazingly sturdy armor.

Choosing Freedom

The truth is that God's armor can't fit on top of our own armor. If you are a *Friends* fan, you might remember the episode where Joey puts on all of Chandler's clothes as retaliation in a fight.[13] He looks ridiculous, like the Stay Puft marshmallow man! Joey can't do anything well with all those clothes on. When we try to put on our own armor through deflecting, hiding, criticizing, masking, we end up not doing anything well over time, and our relationships will suffer. We are lonely because of the barriers between self and God and self and others. Gentleness, compassion, patience, kindness, and humility are hard to practice from a distance. In my story at the beginning, gentleness came from close contact, not from standing at a distance physically or emotionally. **We must come close to one another.**

Coming close is where we see all our weakness, sin, challenges, bad days, up-close wrinkles, cellulite, and pores. But it is also where we see longing, desire, beauty, and strength. This vulnerability is a challenge with others but also with Jesus. It is easy to perform for God, believing that we must clean ourselves up before approaching Him. Recently, I was at a church service and had an experience of Jesus coming close to my attitudes, views, and characteristics that I know are not of Christ. I anticipated His disgust and felt a strong impulse to flee from His holiness and goodness. But He kept coming close, tender and gentle, and His face full of love. The truth is, I am disgusted by these weaknesses, these less-than-perfect parts, and expect the same from Him. But He

---

[13] *"The One Where No One's Ready." Friends*, created by Gail Mancuso, performance by Matt LeBlanc, season 3, episode 2, Bright/Kauffman/Crane Productions and Warner Bros. Television, 1996.

did not express that at all. The tears rolled down my face, and I felt close to panic as I could not breathe at the overwhelming love I felt. I know cognitively that Jesus loves me and accepts all of me. What I didn't realize before this is how much I still try to hide from Him to make myself acceptable. He continues to draw close, and this movement, this gentleness, this love draws me in and I receive His love for a few moments. The release I felt after was freeing and calming, even while still in shock that Jesus would not just think this way about me but demonstrate it so clearly. The experience settled something inside of me, with Jesus leading the way so I could interact more gently with myself and others.

Simple Practices to Shape Us in the New Year

This invitation shapes our interactions toward connection rather than performance. It is an invitation to truly follow Jesus into the new year.

How do we exercise this genuine gentleness as we start? A place to begin is coming close to Jesus, letting Him behold you in His gaze. How does one do that when we cannot SEE Jesus? We are created with holy imaginations, so you are invited to use it here. Imagine sitting at the table or in the chair next to the Trinity; Father, Jesus, and Holy Spirit are there with you, just being with you. Meditate on the words, "chosen people, holy and dearly loved." Don't study them, don't look up other scriptures to support it, but sit in it and allow the Lord's gaze to be on you as His beloved child. Do this for a few minutes daily and see what happens as you allow yourself to experience Him as gentle and compassionate. We must *surrender* to the tenderness and softness. We can be in the presence of love and reject it, resist it, and study it. We can sit in the presence of God, and perform, and deflect, and then leave without truly being transformed in our core by how gentle He is. We can, in His non-shaming presence, ask for His help in removing our old armor. Dane Ortlund says it this way,

> "The yearning heart of God delivers and redelivers sinners who find themselves drowning in the sewage of their life. Whom do you perceive him to be in your sin and your suffering? Who do you think God is, not just on paper, but in the kind of person you believe is hearing you when you pray? How does he feel about you? His saving of us is not cool and calculating, it is a matter of yearning. Not yearning for the Facebook you, the you that you project to everyone around you, not the you that you wish you were, yearning for the real you. The you underneath everything you present to others. We need to understand that however long we've been walking with the Lord, whether we have never read the whole Bible or have a PhD in it, we have a perverse resistance to this. Out of his heart flows mercy, out of our reluctance to receive it. We are the cool and calculating ones, not he. He is open armed. We are stiff armed."[14]

Sitting with Jesus daily helps us know His true heart and His yearning for the real self we hide from Him and others. We, as His people, holy and dearly loved, become clothed with His character as we let ourselves be loved by Him. This

---

[14] Ortlund, Dane. *Gentle and Lowly: The Heart of Christ for Sinners and Sufferers*. Crossway, April 2020.

love and identity serve as protection from the natural hurts of the world and relationships. It is easy to reach for and put on our old clothes, old ways of protection, rather than stay in our new clothes with Jesus' armor. We return, day in and day out, to this intimacy of Jesus' gaze.

Second, we offer our whole selves to Jesus. We speak honestly to Him about our hurts, desires, disappointments, realities we have a hard time accepting, anger toward others or even Him. I don't know about you, but I find myself sometimes praying what I think I should rather than what my heart truly feels. As we talk to Jesus without performing or changing who we are to try to fit His mold, we are more open to being transformed in our heart because we have released our deep wounds, fears, and shame. There is space for the Holy Spirit to fill us with His character and healing as over time He opens his arms to us with gentle mercy, forgiveness, and grace.

Finally, as we empty the burdens, we return to our holy imaginations. Imagine choosing the gentleness of God as clothing and God's armor over that. Imagine putting on our identity as **Redeemed** and **Loved** over our minds, hearts, arms, hands, legs, and feet with the protection God offers. We can move into our world this year in newness of life, reading to engage, serve and love up-close with open arms and not stiff ones. We can share our thoughts with humility, talk openly about a fear with our spouse or friend, honestly respond when we are hurt, apologize authentically, and turn toward others when we would rather turn away. We can do these gently because when we know we are loved and redeemed by God, we can release our hold on perceived needs, outcomes, expectations, and desires.

A Blessing and A Prayer

Beloved one, may you walk in your relationships this year with open gentleness that comes only from the Father, Son, and Holy Spirit who love you with incredible mercy.

Father, would you keep me, Your beloved, strong in You and carried by Your mighty power? Help me to put on Your full armor so that I can stand against the accuser's schemes that cause division, loneliness, and strife. Help me to stand firm in the truth of my identity in Jesus, beloved and named as righteous; that I would be covered from head to foot in Your love so that Your gentleness and mercy overflow to all I encounter. Amen.

Chapter 5

Embracing Strength and Dignity for the New Year: Lessons from Habakkuk

By Rehana De Villiers

"SHE IS CLOTHED WITH STRENGTH AND DIGNITY; SHE CAN LAUGH AT THE DAYS TO COME."
—PROVERBS 31:25

The new year sparks a desire for change, the hope that last year's struggles are indeed behind us. As January 1 rolls around, it offers the crispness of 365 days of different. Yet, reality reminds us that not everything will change or disappear. This year, you may consider new coping strategies or seek advice from friends. But deep down, there's a nagging sense that none of these will genuinely alter the situation or transform how you show up. Before you stop reading, I do believe that learning and strategies have great value. But when we're bone tired from lingering struggles, the last thing we need is more striving. The quote often misattributed to Einstein rings true: doing the same thing repeatedly and expecting different results is insanity.

A Peaceful New Year

I don't know your current struggle(s), but know you are not alone. A reality for the 8.2 billion people currently alive is that everyone faces trials, threats, or temptations.

So, in this chapter, we will do a little Bible study. The Bible is an invaluable source document as we evaluate our plans and priorities, goals, and strategies. In God's Word, we find good and true advice. God's Word shows many examples of people who faced challenges and needed guidance and direction, so it is the perfect place to find suggestions on how to do that as we face a new year and prepare for the next 365 days.

So, let's explore an approach for facing the new year inspired by the biblical Old Testament prophet Habakkuk—a plan and strategy for the new year not filled with desperation and striving but based on dignity and strength.

My Story

Habakkuk was a prophet of God who faced harsh realities. He was distraught, depressed, and doubting his God. I have been where Habakkuk was. In 2015, my family left South Africa to follow God's call to the U.S., leaving our lives and loves behind, including our first grandbaby. We lived in the Chicago suburbs for almost six years, a phase of our family life I have affectionately dubbed the "Midwest Madness."

We faced new challenges, unfamiliar spaces, and unforeseen struggles, from health crises to cultural adjustments. With our family battered by physical, emotional, and spiritual illnesses that ranged from acute to chronic and even life-threatening, life as I expected and hoped for was not working out. The people I was relying on and depending on were not available. Spaces that had previously been places of refuge were unfamiliar, and I had no idea how to navigate them. Often, I wrestled with the question, 'How do I even show up here?'

And the doubts and the distrust in our judgment and decision-making process were plenty. Despite seeking God's guidance through prayer and counsel, I felt lost and overwhelmed. The dream of following God's call felt more like a nightmare. Eventually, I questioned if God was even in it, never mind behind it all. How did I end up here ... in the ruins?

Then, during a Bible study on Habakkuk, I found guidance for facing life's ruins with dignity and strength instead of desperation. His story became a roadmap to a deeper faith. Habakkuk showed me what a life of faith amidst the ruins looks like: a life that recognizes challenges and faces them with dignity and strength, not endless striving and desperation.

Habakkuk's Story

Habakk'uk, a prophet in the 7th century, witnessed rampant societal greed, sin, and injustice in Judah. The Kings of Israel, who were supposed to serve as God's representative rulers both materially and spiritually, were a hot mess. With corrupt leadership, the nation spiraled downward. Exhausted and broken, Habakkuk cried out to God, wanting His intervention. Instead of turning away from God in anger, frustration, apathy, or even atheism, Habakkuk's faith, despite the ruins of his circumstances, propelled him towards God.

There are five lessons to be learned from Habakkuk's story that can be applied to our thinking and preparation for the new year. These lessons show us why and how Habakkuk:
- had honest conversations with God
- rehearsed truths about God
- waited and watched for God's answers
- chose to trust God's promises
- finally gained a perspective shift even if everything fell apart.

These five actions and the choices Habakkuk made help us learn lessons to navigate so we can, too, take actions and make choices for our new year that allow us to move past last year's struggles and stresses and face the new year with strength and dignity.

Lesson 1: Embrace Honest Conversations

In the dramatic opening scene, Habakkuk has a raw and honest dialogue with God. Habakkuk peppers God with questions about His ways and works, evil and punishment, righteousness and justice. God answers His bewildered and baffled, exhausted, and emotional prophet.

Habakkuk's honesty shows us we can bring our unfiltered emotions to God. The Bible, filled with such honest prayers, teaches that these raw conversations, like those of Hannah and Mary and the writers of the 150 Psalms, are vital in our relationship with God.

Habakkuk's Complaints

In Chapter 1, verses 1-4, Habakkuk laments destruction, violence, injustice, greed, strife, and conflict everywhere. He boldly accuses God of inaction and allowing evil to flourish. He questions the effectiveness of God's law and blames God for the suffering of the righteous. Before we judge Habakkuk's boldness, we must reflect on our frustrations. Like him, we often blame God's perceived absence for our trials, turning man's free will into a weapon of accusation and frustration against God.

Habakkuk's Doubts

Like Habakkuk, when God's actions don't align with our expectations, we question His timing, care, and omniscience. Such doubts stem from distress, clouding our understanding of God's love and promises. We put God on trial. During a spiritual desert season or a torrential storm of suffering, like Habakkuk, we ask:

- How long, Lord?
- When, Lord?
- Why, Lord?
- How can you, Lord?
- Don't you know, God?
- Don't you see, God?

Perhaps, like Habakkuk, you have tried to live faithfully to God's instructions for a life that pleases and honors Him. You have done the Bible studies, attended the prayer meetings, and woken up at dawn to pray and journal. You have fasted with a heart genuinely seeking God's intervention and have followed the ten steps to *fill in the blank* ... **yet life is still hard.**

I must note here that these spiritual disciplines hold immense value for our sanctification and suffering because they draw us closer to God, or at least they are supposed to.

I can relate to Habakkuk. I thought moving to the United States to use our gifts and resources for God's Kingdom would make life easier. I would never have admitted my transactional attitude back then, and even now, a glow of embarrassment flashes across my face. I knew better. I know better.

We were never as alone as we had been in those first few years. Rebuilding a life takes time, intentionality, and persistence. And when your soul is weary with the realities of desperate times, in our case, moving across the world, sometimes the energy to do something new gives out. We were weary from the striving, the decisions, the opposition, the disappointments, and the doubts. I felt that conflict and chaos were right around the corner everywhere I looked. And like Habakkuk, I blamed God; I doubted God.

God's Responses

In Chapter 1, verses 5-11, God addresses Habakkuk's doubts not with the answers he desires but with what he needs—the Babylonians are coming as instruments of divine justice. God gives no reason nor makes no excuses to answer Habakkuk's accusations. But God does address the real question that Habakkuk is asking: "Are you going to continue to be silent?" Grace and mercy lie in God's engagement, not in His meeting our expectations.

God's answers often address deeper issues rather than immediate concerns. In the Midwest, God sent unexpected people to unusual places to help in the most unassuming and surprising ways. Random friendships that became a lifeline and continue to enrich my life; a ministry opportunity that stretched me positively and negatively and gave the gift of laborers in women's ministry; a surgical procedure that left me reliant on my husband for weeks that built our struggling marriage into new levels of trust, comfort, and support. Even during disappointments and what seemed like injustices, God reminded me that He is not blind; He takes up my cause, and I can trust Him (Psalm 37). God had His way of using His answers to teach me about myself, my pride, self-reliance, and wrongly-placed hope, even though they were neither the answers, solutions, nor lessons I was looking for.

Whenever we face a new year, we look back on the past one, and often, that brings up painful memories, problems, regrets, and disappointments. We examine and question the times when God was silent, and we felt stranded, or when God moved in one direction completely opposite to where we were heading. And this can leave us feeling defeated, despondent, or anxious about planning goals and setting new intentions. When God's answers don't match our desires, we face a choice: trust His plan or cling to our understanding, methods, and timing. Trusting God requires believing in His promises and purposes, even when circumstances remain difficult. Ultimately, we wrestle with the question, "Don't you care, God?" feeling far from the royal identity we know we hold. Yet, in these moments, we must lean into faith, embracing a perspective of trust and hope.

God as Mystery

I came to know Jesus on the eve of my 30th birthday. I remember being awed by God's patience and presence. I wrestled with the tension that God is personal, knowable, approachable, and accessible (His immanence) but also wholly other and outside of what we can ultimately know, understand, or experience (His transcendence). There'll always be an element of mystery to God.

And this is good news. I have heard many Bible teachers say that it is fitting to have some mystery about God because we don't want to worship a God who can be mastered and manipulated. We want to worship a God who can be trusted.

Action Steps:

- What question, concern, frustration, or fear about this past year or the year to come do you need to get honest with God about?
- Where do you need to reconcile that God's answers may not align with the answer(s) you are hoping for or expecting?
- How are you putting God on trial for situations you faced in the past or you may face in the new year?
- What responses are evoked when you read about God's kindness, mercy, and grace to answer His frustrated and fearful servant?

Lesson 2: Rehearse Truths about God

After expressing frustration and receiving an unsettling response, Habakkuk takes the next step to deeper faith: he pauses to recall truths about God. As an Israelite familiar with God's promises to the patriarchs and covenants of faithfulness God made, Habakkuk draws from his heritage, referencing God's ancient deeds. This reflection was vital because it reoriented his understanding. Habakkuk had to re-evaluate his theology and reorient his mind and heart to not what he thought but how God revealed Himself.

Who God Is

In Habakkuk 1:12, the prophet's descriptions of God influence his view of God.

> Are you not from eternity, LORD my God?
> My Holy One, you will not die.
> LORD, you appointed them to execute judgment;
> my Rock, you destined them to punish us.
> —Habakkuk 1:12 CSB (emphasis added)

Habakkuk refers to God as being from eternity, meaning God stands outside the concept of time. He has no beginning nor an end. So, God is not subject to the limits of time and instead holds time (Psalm 31:5). Then Habakkuk speaks to the LORD, my God, using the covenant name of God, Yahweh, the God of Israel who had proved Himself faithful to covenants made with them. Habakkuk also refers to God as My Holy One, emphasizing that only Yahweh is genuinely God and is completely set apart from other artificial deities. He is the sacred, Living God. And because God is holy, He alone is righteous in his actions, specifically in Habakkuks's context, as Judah's righteous judge.

Habakkuk repeatedly affirms his relationship with God and that God is his Rock, his place of refuge for safety and strength during threat and trial.

The Importance of Rehearsing Truths

For Habakkuk, remembering these truths was vital, especially as Judah faced impending judgment. Many would struggle with their faith in a good God amidst terrible challenges. Habakkuk knew that to make it, he needed the stability of the truth of who God is. We, too, face challenges where God's actions—or apparent inactions—don't make sense, and we feel alone, misunderstood, isolated, and that God has never shown up for us. In these moments, recalling who God is becomes our lifeline. Whether you've witnessed answered prayers or are struggling to feel God's presence, remembering God's character can renew your strength.

A new year is an exciting time but also scary. The calendar days hold both good and bad possibilities that either move us ahead, grind us to a screeching halt, or set us back for a while. There is no way to know how the year will pan out. Rehearsing the stabilizing truth of who God is means that we can face the exciting yet unknown new year with a strength that comes not from our own skill or strategy but from the fact that God's character is stable and that He can be trusted.

Rehearsing truths about God can be a brutal exercise during desperate times. Yet, God understands our frailty (Psalm 103:14). That's why He's provided a written record of His redemptive work, revealing His restorative involvement in humanity's story—from creation to the fulfillment of salvation through Jesus Christ and to the establishment and spread of the Christian faith gathered in local communities globally, which includes all humanity and looks forward to the ultimate consummation of God's redemptive plan.

Whether you've grown up immersed in God's truths or are new to faith, rehearsing His attributes can be transformative. Resources like Bible studies or a quick online search for "attributes of God" can provide lists of His qualities to meditate on.

Action Steps:
- What truths about God can you rehearse?
- Find a resource that lists the attributes of God.
- What attributes of God do you need to draw strength from for the new year?
- What actions of God over the past few years can you gain hope for the new year?
- Memorize these scriptures that remind you of who God is.

Lesson 3: Waiting and Watching

In Habakkuk chapter 2, we see a framework for navigating uncertainty and waiting that serves as a third lesson to a deep faith despite the ruins. Scripture offers numerous examples of waiting. Abraham waited years for his promised child; Joseph waited decades for his dreams to come true; the Israelites endured centuries in Egypt before their deliverance. The Hebrew exiles would wait 40 years before entering their Promised Land. Figures like Hannah and David showed perseverance in waiting. Anna, widowed young, had waited her whole life worshiping in the Temple, looking forward to the Messiah. Even today, the Church waits for Christ's return. Waiting is a critical component of the faith journey.

The Struggle with Waiting

For me, waiting can feel like being stuck. My decision-making is fraught with overthinking and hesitation, which can lead to procrastination. It's tempting to rely on quick fixes: seeking advice, researching solutions, or creating endless plans. However, actual waiting involves trusting God's timing and direction.

The start of any new year holds so much promise that we don't want to sit around and wait. We want to get busy shaping these expectations into realities sooner rather than later. Waiting seems an awful lot like a waste of precious time to me, and maybe it does to you, too. But waiting well is needed if we want to know how to move forward with God's wisdom and guidance instead of our own so our new year will be shaped by God and we can face it with strength and dignity. Waiting well is a skill we need to learn to hear from God. Waiting well is a skill I am working on.

Habakkuk's Framework for Waiting

Waiting on God requires patience. Habakkuk shows us that patient waiting on God is active, not passive. Habakkuk:

- adopts a posture of readiness, emphasizing standing firm, remaining stationed, and keeping watch.
- is at a designated place on the city wall, positioned to see and hear from God.
- is preparing to dialogue with God mentally, emotionally, and spiritually.

Preparation and Awe

As we wait, we must prepare ourselves to see and hear from God, as Habakkuk did. Preparation is a crucial aspect of waiting. My mentor often encourages us to "Prepare to be Amazed," emphasizing the need to clear our minds of doubts and ready ourselves to witness God's work. This preparation involves dusting the cobwebs off truths we learned, emptying the trash of untruths we've believed, and cultivating an open heart. This preparation also means intentionally positioning and posturing yourself so you can step away from the grit of daily life to cultivate awe and wonder. For me, that is being in nature.

Nature inspires awe and amazement in me. The deafening roar of ocean waves that lap to and fro on sun-kissed golden sands leaves me in awe at the power and force of the ocean that belies worlds teeming with marine life existing at depths that man may never be able to reach and explore. The blue-gray rise of majestic mountains with ravines, valleys, and waterfalls carved in precision and filled with fauna and flora as diverse as the environments these rocky giants tower over leave me speechless. I am amazed and in awe at the juxtaposition of the splendor, majesty, and magnificence of the ocean and mountains with my life's commonness and plainness.

Focus Shift

Habakkuk's intentional approach highlights the importance of shifting focus from problems to God. Instead of being consumed by his desperate circumstances, he trusted God's sovereignty, actively sought God's guidance, and intentionally invited God into his situation.

As New Testament believers, we have the indwelling Holy Spirit, who comforts, teaches, and reminds us of God's truths (John 14:25-26). The Spirit helps us live guided and less guarded and helps us navigate our trials by shifting our questions from "Why is this happening?" to "What is God teaching me?"

Action Steps:

- Decide on a place in your home where you can purposefully posture yourself to wait for God this new year.
- Find an activity that intentionally helps you to focus on God more than on the trial.
- What actions or attitudes from last year have you developed that may mean you are living guarded and maybe even becoming angered or alienated?
- How can you invite the Holy Spirit into your new year to guide you?

Lesson 4: Choose to Trust God's Promises

One of the critical lessons God teaches us is perseverance through trust because we can trust Him even when, especially if, our circumstances don't change immediately. Habakkuk shows us this in Chapter 2, as God instructs him to write a message of assurance.

A Faithful Message

God's message would be a 'witness' to what God had determined would happen, a confirmation and testimony of how this story would unfold. So, the delayed message was trustworthy and reliable. Habakkuk and his peers would know that the fulfillment of God's word would happen the way God wanted and in His exact manner and timing. In Habakkuk 2:4b, God reminds Habakkuk that "the person of integrity will live because of his faithfulness." God is calling His prophet and His people to persevere in faithfulness.

Despite facing injustice and impending Babylonian oppression, the righteous are assured of preservation because they trust God's promises. And so Habakkuk learns to cultivate a mindset that places joy in God, regardless of external chaos. Habakkuk begins to reinforce his God-confidence because faith is not about perfect understanding but about our perseverance and trust, about our faithfulness to believe the promised words of the Perfect One.

Transformed to Faithfulness

I have lived enough decades with myself to know the limits of my faithfulness. Praise be to Jesus that it is *not* our faithfulness or righteousness that we have to rely on. As New Testament believers in Jesus Christ, we are made righteous because of His righteousness and are helped in faithfulness by His faithfulness (Romans 5:1, Philippians 3:9, Romans 3:21-26).

The perseverance we need to develop comes not from our skillset or character traits but from a hope that does not disappoint (Romans 5:5) based on the covenantal love and faithfulness received through salvation by faith in Jesus Christ and the sanctification and regeneration work of the indwelling Holy Spirit.

Jesus, as the Righteous and Faithful One (Revelation 19:11), places His righteousness on us; it is how God sees us. Our sanctification involves God shaping us daily, molding our imperfect hearts to reflect Christ more closely. Our stability and integrity come from His faithfulness, not our own.

Assured of Faithfulness

Yet, we struggle with sinful habits and strongholds and are surrounded by sinful people and places. God knows that trust is hard for us. God knows we need reassurance. The Bible overflows with promises of eternal life and joy for believers (1 John 5:11-12; Romans 8:38-39). It also addresses our earthly fears, anxieties, burdens, weaknesses, and struggles, assuring us of His presence, purpose, and power (Isaiah 41:10; Romans 8:28; Jeremiah 29:11; Philippians 4:6-7; John 10:28-29; Psalm 46:1; Matthew 11:28-30; Romans 8:38-39; 2 Corinthians 12:9; Psalm 23:4). The Bible gives eternal assurances and earthly promises of God's faithful presence, good purposes, and unrivaled power.

In Chapter 2, Habakkuk is given assurances that God is neither asleep nor unaware. And even though the impending Babylonian invasion is imminent, it is not outside God's control or purview. While the Babylonians may be renowned and feared across the ancient world, the day will come when the whole earth will recognize that God is the mighty One and will be speechless. God reminded Habakkuk that He is greater than any army, nation, or evil on the horizon.

The Bigger Picture

This echoes what we read in Revelation, which unveils history's end and the return of our King Jesus, the Lord of Armies, who will return to set all things right, destroy His enemies, and restore His people. Though filled with imagery and symbolism, Revelation offers hope to believers enduring suffering. It reminds us of God's ultimate victory and the secure salvation of His people. Many believers experiencing intense suffering and persecution have found refuge in Revelation, which builds their trust in perseverance. A life of faith requires a deliberate choice to seek out and place our trust in God's promises, especially in God's process, because His thoughts are not like ours, and His ways are not ours (Isaiah 55:8-9). Understanding the bigger picture builds our God-confidence, even when our present circumstances seem overwhelming.

Action Steps:

- Which challenges or difficulties from last year(s) have consumed your thoughts?
- Write down God's promises and assurances that resonate with you and make them visible in your daily life to remind you and build your God-confidence. You could use beautifully simple and personal scribbled sticky notes or beautifully designed and professional scripture cards bought online.
- Choose a mindset shift you choose to cultivate as a goal for the new year: finding moments of joy, actively choosing trust, and persevering despite your challenging realities.
- Thank Jesus daily for His righteousness and faithfulness, and to help you rely on that for the new year.
- Reflect on and memorize Isaiah 55:8-9 to find peace, hope, and trust in a powerful, good God.

Lesson 5: Perspective Shift

Habakkuk starts and ends with unchanged circumstances, but transformation has occurred. The prophet was lamenting and complaining and seemed almost defiant. But as the book ends, Habakkuk moves to purposeful surrender, as seen in his prayer in Chapter 3—a lament wrapped in a praise song. In Chapter 3, verse 1, Habakkuk acknowledges that his understanding of God has deepened after his vulnerable and honest conversation with Him: "I stand in awe of your deeds." Habakkuk's faith has gone from academic or rote to experiential.

Lament to Praise

His prayer in Chapter 3, verses 2-15, praises God's majesty, power, and wisdom, recalling God's past acts of salvation on behalf of His people from bondage and slavery in Egypt.

Initially questioning God's inaction, Habakkuk now sees God's presence in his life, and he shifts from despair to worship. Habakkuk was able to deeply feel and know that just like God was active in the lives of His people in days past, God was active in his time. Habakkuk shifted, even though his circumstances and challenges did not.

Sometimes, God's answers, timing, and methods to our laments and challenges do not make sense until we see things differently. This perspective shift—from pacing in anxiety to waiting in worship—is what we all need when life feels overwhelming.

Strength and Dignity

In verses 16-19 of Chapter 3, we see more evidence of Habakkuk's perspective shift. He acknowledges that even if his worst fears are realized and everything falls apart, his faith in God would not.

The "yet I will celebrate..." of verse 18 shows Habakkuk choosing faith by clinging to the source of his strength to face his fears. This echoes Proverbs 31:25, a scripture I have often gravitated to.

"She is clothed with strength and dignity; she can laugh at the days to come."

It takes great faith to face an uncertain future, an uncertain new year, with joy and confidence. When we are in deep pain or trouble, laughing without fear of the future seems almost like insanity. It requires a transformation of thought, a renewing of the mind (Romans 12:2), but more than that, it requires a shifted orientation of how we live.

In Ephesians 4:22-24 Paul tells us to put off the old self and embrace the new, reflecting God's righteousness and holiness. Paul is teaching us to shift away from relying on old strategies and systems of self and instead rely on Christ and trust in God's established character and proven actions. When making intentions and goals for the new year, we often focus a lot on doing and less so on being. But the Christian life is about being a new person, a person molded in Christ's image, reliant on and reflecting Him. This may mean a renovation of our priorities and plans for the new year for ourselves and our families. It might mean re-evaluating what activities we sign our kids up for, which friendships and relationships we choose to pursue, and which battles we choose to fight or leave in God's hands. The new year might be calling for new perspectives of trust and faithfulness.

Habakkuk's Trusted Hope

And here we take our leave of Habakkuk. He is facing some bitter realities, yet he has a deep and dignified trust, a trust not built on circumstances or cookie-cutter solutions, a faith rooted in God's sovereign, powerful, and purposeful character. Habakkuk realized that he could not measure God's faithfulness or goodness based on his circumstances because his circumstances were steeped in brokenness. His perspective changed from asking, "Where are you, God?" to declaring, "I know you are at work." Habakkuk would wait and watch God at work instead of watching the chaos around him.

Habakkuk's trust in God is echoed by Job, who, despite significant loss, trusted God's authority and sovereignty and proclaimed,

"The Lord gives, and the Lord takes away.
Blessed be the name of the Lord."
—Job 1:21b CSB

Similarly, Jeremiah, a contemporary of Habakkuk, found hope in God's unfailing love and new mercies.

"Yet I call this to mind, and therefore, I have hope:
Because of the Lord's faithful love, we do not perish,
for his mercies never end.
They are new every morning; great is your faithfulness!
I say, "The Lord is my portion; therefore,
I will put my hope in him."
The Lord is good to those who wait for him,
to the person who seeks him.
It is good to wait quietly for salvation from the Lord."
—Lamentations 3:21-26 CSB

And like the psalmist, we can face the new year because "God is our refuge and strength, an ever-present help in trouble" (Psalm 46:1, ESV). God tells us to

> "... Be still, and know that I am God.
> I will be exalted among the nations,
> I will be exalted in the earth!" (Psalm 46:10, ESV).

Action Steps:

- Journal where you have been relying on yourself instead of resting in Christ this past year.
- In which circumstances do you need to shift your focus to develop trust in God's faithfulness and goodness and ask Him to help you do that?
- Regularly be still and acknowledge God's presence and activity in your life.
- Ask God to calm your anxious heart with assurances of his activity.
- Meditate on Psalm 46 and Lamentations 3:21–26.

Our Trusted Hope

Habakkuk's hope in his chaos rested on who God is. When we process our feelings and pain through the lens of sound theology of who God is, it aligns our feelings and thinking and brings hope. We can cry out to God, not in despair, but with the assurance of His faithfulness. Coming to God with bold expressions of our pain, anguish, and confusion becomes a healthy and holy activity. Habakkuk's perspective shifted from all that was wrong and evil to the One who is Righteous and True. Our faith in Jesus is the balm of peace for our troubled hearts (John 14:1, 27).

Promise Keeper

As I have been writing this chapter, the lyrics of Hope Darst's "Promise Keeper" resonated deeply:

"I'll see Your goodness in the land of the Living,
I'll see Your goodness right here, right now.
Cause You know the ending before the beginning
I know that You have worked all things out."[15]

Like Habakkuk, we can be new people as we head into a new year, with profound and dignified faith amidst and despite the ruins.

Like Habakkuk, we can face the new year with courage and confidence.

Like Habakkuk, we can say come what may, we can choose to believe, worship, turn to, and find joy in Jesus, our true salvation, our Promise Keeper.

Like Habakkuk, we can trust God with this new year because the Sovereign Lord is our strength and dignity.

Selah.

---

[15] Darst, Hope. "Promise Keeper." *Peace Be Still*, Fair Trade Services, 2020. http://smarturl.it/HopeDarstPKSF/spotify.

Chapter 6

Building a Firm Foundation: Achieving Better Health in the New Year and Beyond

By Lindsay Koach

"HEALTH IS NOT SIMPLY BEING FREE OF MENTAL AND PHYSICAL DISEASE; IT IS A WHOLENESS OF MIND AND BODY, WHICH LETS US LIVE OUR LIVES TO THE FULLEST. AS CHRISTIANS, WE KNOW GOD CALLS US TO HONOR HIM WITH OUR BODIES (1 CORINTHIANS. 6:20). THE HEALTH OF OUR PHYSICAL BODIES IS TIED TO OUR EMOTIONAL, MENTAL, AND SPIRITUAL HEALTH."[16]

Lessons From My Health Journey

Are there things in our lives that are just as, or maybe more, important than food and exercise when it comes to being healthy? Yes.

When my health was at its worst ten years ago, I experienced a shift in my understanding of what being healthy means. This came about by working with an Integrative Nutrition Health Coach, Frederick, who had me do self-reflection exercises and study the pillars of holistic health.

---

[16] Adventist Church, Seventh Day. "A Definition of Health." *In Step With Jesus | A Closer Walk 1*, 2016, https://tinyurl.com/mr3wp7sd.

What I discovered through those times of reflection and learning was that being healthy is all-encompassing. It's not something we can break up into parts; everything is connected. In the beginning of healing my hypothyroidism and hormonal imbalance, I placed a lot of focus on the foods, drinks, supplements, and workouts, but I wasn't paying as close attention to spirituality, relationships, and how career or life work highly influences physical health. These areas of life are known as primary foods (along with movement), coined by Joshua Rosenthal, founder of the Institute for Integrative Nutrition.

When we are lacking faith, not feeling supported, or working in a career or work path that drains us, this negatively impacts our physical health. Learning how my own primary food "deficiencies" were contributing to my thyroid and hormone imbalance, I quickly began to understand where I lacked "nutrition" and what areas of my life needed to be "fed."

For example, I thought I was doing ok in the spiritual area with my Christian faith. We regularly attended church, my husband and I both helped with various committees, and I taught Sunday school and volunteered in many ways. The thing is, I wasn't spending quality alone time with God each day. I wasn't filling up my "faith cup" with His wisdom.

The same went for my marriage. I thought my husband and I had a healthy relationship, but we weren't giving each other the proper nourishment we needed to thrive as a couple. We allowed distractions to trump our commitments and ultimately left each other feeling more unsupported than we realized. I wasn't making time to see friends or be with other moms. I was experiencing challenges within some family relationships, which brought stress and depression. All of these things contributed to my "relationship cup" being empty, which depleted me in different ways.

At this time, I was primarily at home taking care of my one-year-old son. As much as I love being a mom, I realized through self-reflection that I needed my own time too. I had a bad habit of putting myself on the back burner and not attending to my own needs, which left me feeling resentful at times or just burnt out. I don't have certain components of a typical support system, so Frederick helped me get creative in obtaining the support I needed and have time to take care of myself.

After I started working on these energetic areas of my life, I physically started feeling better. I was still focusing on healthy foods, drinks, and movement, and this physical nourishment fueled me to be my best in the roles connected to my primary foods. The interconnectedness continued to show itself, and I knew I was on the path to healing. Eventually, I experienced physical proof of this: I became pregnant when I was told that wouldn't happen again! I also had an unmedicated vaginal birth after cesarean after experiencing a traumatic labor and delivery with my first baby. When my second baby was nine months old, I found out I was pregnant again. God is good, and His design works as intended when we get to the root of the problem.

Laying the Groundwork

Many people, especially women, look to the fresh start of the new year as a time to commit to better health practices. We tend to jump into new eating plans, exercise programs, or other health and wellness modalities with hopes of achieving weight loss, higher energy, or maybe overcoming a specific health issue.

With over ten years of experience in health coaching and my own healing journey, I find that many people become overwhelmed with their health goals because they have not been properly communicated to those closest to them. This leads to not having proper support. Without support in place, the exercise can't be maintained long-term, and the new ways of eating may create isolation, which leads to giving up. Also, without understanding how our physical, mental, emotional, and spiritual health is connected, motivation and inspiration are lost. It doesn't have to be this way.

The process of identifying the root causes of our health challenges and implementing realistic solutions starts with a foundation of open communication and support from God and our loved ones. Before we get to the guidance on that, let's look at some information on our physical, mental, emotional, and spiritual health. These points will be great to bring up when you have a sit-down conversation with your family or loved ones who will be alongside you on this journey.

Physical Health

Food

Our food supply and way of eating has drastically changed since the industrialization of food and introduction of ultra-processed foods. Most of what we find in a typical grocery store is what I call "empty food." These are products that are found in boxes, cans, and other containers where the food has been modified, engineered, or heavily processed with chemicals, additives, and industrial solvents that degrade the quality of the food. This is not the way we are intended to receive nutrition. God has given us the fruits of this earth and dominion over the animals. Our foods should have a root or a mother and be stewarded with the intended growing conditions and care.

People will always ask me about calories. "How much should I eat?" What's more important is the quality of the food, the way different types of foods are combined on our plate and the timing of our meals and snacks. The quality of our food could be a chapter in itself, but the idea is to have foods in their purest, most natural form without chemicals or modification. We will discuss that more later. With combining foods, it's best to have your plate be roughly 30% protein, 30% healthy fat, and 40% complex carbohydrates such as vegetables, fruits, and whole grains (naturally gluten-free ones are great). When it comes to timing, eating the bulk of your food earlier in the day and eating less as the day winds down is a successful action step for improved health. Our bodies digest food best when the sun is up. As the sun sets, so does our ability to digest and assimilate nutrients. That's why people find themselves with indigestion after a heavy dinner later in the evening. The body can't process food as well at that time.

YOUR IDEAL PLATE

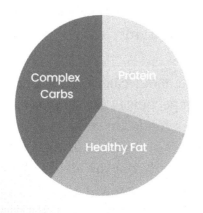

- **Protein (30%)**
  Key words for animal protein are grass-fed, pasture-raised, organic, and soy-free. Non-GMO is good, but organic is best. Plants such as hemp hearts, edamame, tofu, tempeh, legumes, chickpeas, lima beans, cauliflower, and potatoes are great.

- **Healthy Fat (30%)**
  Animal fats such as grass-fed butter, ghee, tallow, and lard are good choices. For plant-based fats, add nuts and seeds. Try avocado with your meals, or avocado oil for cooking. Coconut oil and olive oil are great too. All oils should be cold-pressed.

- **Complex Carbs (40%)**
  Think in terms of vegetables, fruits, and wholesome grains that are organic. Look for naturally gluten-free alternatives to wheat like quinoa, rice, millet, or amaranth. Homemade sourdough bread is great too.

Movement

When it comes to exercise and the new year, most people will commit to a fitness program that is strict and includes movement that they don't enjoy. This is a mistake. Look for something that you actually *want to do* and look forward to. As your journey progresses, you can challenge yourself with different types of workouts. In the beginning, the important thing to do is pick something that you actually want to do and feel motivated to stick with.

As a mom of three, I want to be sure to caution all moms to take care of any pelvic floor issues before exercising. I was anxious to get back to the gym a few years ago, and I did further damage to the separation in my abdominal wall (diastasis recti). Schedule a consultation with a physical therapist who can treat pelvic floor challenges. You may be like me and need pelvic floor exercises before starting anything else or while starting a new exercise program.

Mental, Emotional, and Spiritual Health

The Physical Health Connection

Let's talk about the physical connection to our mental, emotional, and spiritual health. One important component of this is the community of microorganisms that are present in our bellies. You may have heard the buzz phrase "gut health." That's because the health of our gut is a cornerstone of our overall health. 80% of our immune system resides there, and brain chemicals are made in our gut. If we are eating junk foods, then we will experience junk moods. Eating whole, unadulterated foods and drinks encourages the growth of better-quality bacteria and building materials for our blood, cells, tissues, and beyond. Creating healthier environments affects our microbiome as well, and it's important to expose ourselves to the outside world as much as possible. Hiking, gardening, or just playing in the dirt helps keep our gut and overall body, mind, and spirit resilient.

WHY WE NEED A HEALTHY GUT

WHEN OUR GUT IS HEALTHY, OUR OVERALL HEALTH IS BETTER.

DID YOU KNOW?
WHEN YOUR GUT IS HEALTHY, YOUR SKIN IS CLEAR AND GLOWING!

H HORMONE HEALTH
- A healthy gut means healthy hormone production and balance. The microbiome is the cornerstone of these processes.

P PREVENTION OF CHRONIC HEALTH CONDITIONS
- Poor gut health is linked to many chronic health conditions. Rebuilding damaged gut lining and balancing bacteria heals many chronic digestive issues and varying health disorders.

B BRAIN HEALTH
- Neurotransmitters like seratonin are made in the gut. A healthy gut means better moods and feelings!

I IMMUNE HEALTH
- 80% of our immune system resides in our gut. Healthier guts mean less seasonal sickness and more resilience against illnesses.

Additionally, when we take in poor foods and drinks, we cloud our spiritual connection. I have personally experienced this. Various cultures believe that clean intake of foods, drinks, and herbs enhances the gateway to the spiritual realm. There are studies that show our pineal gland becomes calcified by taking in substances like fluoride and many of the chemicals that we find in drinking water and processed food.[17] This is detrimental because the pineal gland plays a part in regulating our circadian rhythm, melatonin production and can influence mood, energy levels, and overall well-being. Some spiritual practices link this gland to intuition, perception, and spiritual enlightenment. When I am taking better care of myself physically, I feel strengthened in my spiritual health. Do you?

---

[17] Belay, Daniel Gashaneh, and Misganaw Gebrie Worku. "Prevalence of Pineal Gland Calcification: Systematic Review and Meta-Analysis." *Systematic Reviews*, U.S. National Library of Medicine, 6 Mar. 2023, pmc.ncbi.nlm.nih.gov/articles/PMC9987140.

The Human Experience Connection

What elements of our human experience affect our mental, emotional, and spiritual health? Let's start with spiritual health, which is a pillar of strength in many healthy people's lives. Having faith and living a spiritual practice is seen as a stronghold in many cultures all over the world for well-being and longevity. That's why it is deemed a "primary food" by Joshua Rosenthal, founder of the Institute for Integrative Nutrition (as described at the beginning of this chapter). When we are spiritually healthy, we are focused on a greater power of love and grace. We possess a readiness to serve and love from that wellspring of goodness. A health-related factor in the wellness of those who are spiritually steadfast are the relationships that come with faith. People tend to connect with others who are like-minded and bond with their faith-based community. Collectively, they are living for something that is positive and encouraging, and together they complete tasks, projects, and other initiatives to better themselves and their community.

Spiritually healthy people tend to have an easier time with consistency and putting the work into difficult projects because they allow themselves to be guided by faith. They know and understand the fruits of labor because those who have a spiritual practice have usually encountered difficulties and had uphill battles where faith got them through. Additionally, mental clarity and strength are common among those who are spiritually inclined. If you've had lengthy conversations with individuals who have strong faith, you can see those qualities. For example, I believe in God, and I am a Christian. At the end of the day, I know His love and grace will see me through. No matter what I face, I know I have steadfast support in the Lord and in heaven. I can lean on Him and His wisdom. I have choices, and I do my best, but ultimately, everything is in the Lord's hands. My mental and physical health are positively affected by these empowering thoughts and conclusions I gather from reading holy scripture and maintaining a relationship with Jesus. How has spirituality affected your health and well-being? Have you had positive or negative experiences? Have you drifted from being spiritually active? I know I have at times, and this is something that regularly comes up as a missing puzzle piece for others who are struggling to regain their health and well-being.

Next, let's look at relationships; also a primary food. If we don't experience the love and relational connection we need, then we lack internal resources to maintain better health and well-being. For example, most of the individuals I have worked with do not have a present and supportive mother. This is something that may be overlooked when it comes to health and wellbeing, but it's vitally important. For example, a woman having her first baby with the support of a nurturing and present mother of her own makes a huge difference in a young mother's health. During that first year with the baby, there are so many events that physically, mentally, and spiritually challenge a new mother. Having that maternal nourishment to help a woman navigate that season impacts every level of health for her and the baby. What about spouses or partners? If they don't take interest in what your needs or desires are, then how can you feel supported in your endeavors? Additionally, couples share routines and daily practices within the home. Your lives are intertwined. If your partner is out of sync with you, it makes it very difficult to make the necessary lifestyle changes to achieve health goals. This is another pain point I've worked through with my clients, and success is possible if everyone is willing to communicate and work together.

    Lastly, let's look at our careers and life work. If we work in situations that drain us and drag us down, this will affect our health and wellness on every level. I have personally been in situations where my job was making me unwell. It is incredibly burdensome to experience that, and above all, it defines a factor found in many health problems: chronic stress. We know that when people have chronic stress, they have a higher chance of disease. When you look at the word "disease," you can see DIS-EASE: a state of dis-ease or not being at ease. We obviously don't live in a utopia and can't escape stress entirely. Stress can be good, but when it's chronic due to a career or work situation that is gnawing at us, then it's time to make a change. It's important to check in with yourself and reflect. So many times, people will shove negative feelings down and keep pressing on. In the long term, this isn't going to fare well. When we are chronically stressed, we tend to have shallow breathing, don't digest food well, get sick more often, wrestle with low energy, have sleep issues, low libido, and hold a lot of tension. People will rely on stimulants like caffeine to keep their energy and focus or fall to depressants like alcohol to relax and disengage from their thoughts. Working at a job that chronically drains or stresses you may hinder the motivation to cook healthy food, exercise, or just take care of yourself properly. Can you see where this is going? Everything is a trickle-down effect, and this is especially true for career/life work.

On the flipside, there are examples where people want a change in their work or are at home and want to work outside of the home. One example is women who are having trouble with being at home full-time with their children. They may feel like they need a job or something to do aside from being a parent, and that's ok. Finding a balance and feeling like you have healthy boundaries is what matters. If you don't, then it's time to consider your options. An Integrative Nutrition Health Coach like me helps clients make changes in these areas just as much as food and exercise. Many times, those elements are a priority because they lead to people having better ability to physically take care of themselves.

Creating a Support System

Now, let's get to the new year action plan! Our first step is creating support. Without proper support in place, it's difficult to make headway with health goals. First, let's reflect on what your current support system looks like. Follow the questions below to make a quick assessment.

Support System Reflection

- What is your current support system? Is a relationship with God a part of your support system?
- If you have children, when people discuss having a village or that motherhood takes a village, what feelings come up for you? How would you describe your village?
- When you think of your ideal support system, what do you envision?
- What are three steps you could take now to start building that ideal support system?

- Sometimes, we think something will be supportive, but then once we're in it, we see that it's not. It may even become a source of negative feelings. Are there boundaries you need to put in place or people/groups/platforms you feel you need to cut out or reduce time with to make yourself feel better?

The Investor Presentation

Now that you have done some reflection on your support system and we've reviewed important points regarding health that can be discussed with your family or loved ones, it is imperative to establish a meeting. This is the opportunity to voice hopes and create interconnected support to make results happen. It is also an opportunity for you to make your case that if you can feel your best, then you will serve your best. This is also a prime opportunity to pray together as a family over your goals and create intentions.

This is what I fondly call The Investor Presentation. This is truly a calling for those who love you to show up so that you can show up for them. We are talking about the most important investments: health, happiness, and a bright future. Here are some guidelines for this call to action meeting with your family or those who live with you and will be alongside you on this health journey:

- Set this up for success by telling them that you are embarking on a journey to improve your health. It will positively impact their lives, too, and they can join you! You just need some help from everyone to see it through, or do this together and be accountability partners. This is a good time to pray as a family/team.

- Declare your intentions and explain what you're doing and why you're doing it. It's important that you express to them that you're doing this for them as much as for yourself. Your intention is wanting to be a better partner, parent, employee, etc., and fulfill your roles with energy and clarity. It's not just about your health but about everyone having a better quality of life in your home.
- Let them know you'll be following guidelines for eating better and making better lifestyle choices but that this is not a diet. It's a new way to look at food and self-care as medicine and an adventure. This is supposed to be fun, and it's going to positively impact everyone.
- Explain that you will be implementing positive changes to making the home environment healthier and reducing toxins/chemicals in personal care products.
- Share that you will be looking closer at areas of life that feed you, and everyone should join in this reflection. You will look at faith, relationships, career, hobbies, and exercise.
- This isn't going to be perfect, and it's not meant to be. There will be times everything is clicking and times that it's tough. It's a journey, and asking for God's guidance and supporting one another will make it more enjoyable and successful.
- Then, finally, start discussing the importance of delegating tasks, which creates an important layer of support for everyone. You can't do all the household tasks, errands, running kids to practices/games,

school work, etc., while taking on improving your health and the health of your family. This part is up to you in how you want to communicate or delegate different tasks, or part of the "mental load" you carry at home. It will take some time to figure out how this will come together, but get the conversation started and give yourselves a deadline to have a plan in place.

The Plan to Get Healthier

When it comes to focusing on the action steps, these are general guidelines that I share with others when they are ready to experience better overall health. Everyone is different, but these guidelines are known to improve energy levels, reduce aches and pains, improve sleep, help weight loss, regulate bowel movements, clear up skin, and help balance hormones.

After you have met with your family and had the necessary conversation around everyone's hopes and goals for the new year, you can have a second sit-down meeting to go over these guidelines.

Spirituality

Make time to pray, read Scripture, or do a daily spiritual devotional. First thing in the morning is a great way to set the day, or maybe the last thing at night is better for you. Pick what will work and be realistic for you with your schedule. Having your faith and your relationship with God is going to be your anchor that will keep you grounded and focused on achieving the action steps that I will lay out next.

Food

Slowly take the ultra-processed foods out of the house. If you want to keep snacks and packaged foods, read labels and be aware of the quality. Focus on having more vegetables, fruits, sources of protein, fermented foods, and get away from sugary foods and drinks. The idea is to "crowd out" the bad with the good. Remember that meals need protein, healthy fat, and complex carbohydrates. Use natural sweeteners like raw honey, real maple syrup from trees, dates or date paste, coconut sugar, or monk fruit sweetener. Stevia is ok, too, but make sure it's just Stevia. Avoid GMOs (genetically modified organisms) and go organic as much as possible. Organic means non-GMO and free of chemical fertilizers, pesticides, and other artificial agents. If you don't already filter your drinking water and bathing water, now is a good time to start.

Food and Mood

Keep a food mood journal. This does not have to be fancy. Simply keep a notebook with you and write down how you feel after you eat every meal. Try to do this for two weeks. Make sure you write down how you feel after you have something that isn't healthy. This reminds you of why you're doing what you're doing and helps you to see if there's certain foods that bother you. It can also alert you if you made a bad food combination. For example, too much caffeine and not enough protein gives me a bad headache.

Food Prep and Relationships

Prep food together as a family for the week on a weekend day where you have a window of time to do so. This is your family's time to be together and get food ready for the week. Make it fun! Play music, catch up on the week, and learn new things in the kitchen. There is a direct correlation between preparing food ahead of time and having success with health goals like weight loss.

Movement

Commit to two to three days of exercise for at least 20 minutes. Choose something that you love to do. It can be a Zumba class or an online workout on YouTube that you can do in your own house. Make it something that is realistic to do and brings you JOY. We don't want moaning and groaning... too much.

Personal Care and Cleaning

Try to pay more attention to what is in your personal care products and household cleaning items. We want to get away from chemicals because they raise estrogen and contribute to cancers. Look closely at your body wash, shampoo and conditioner, body lotion, and makeup. Are these brands committed to removing things like parabens, phthalates, or any other unhealthy ingredients? Seek out brands that are removing endocrine disrupting chemicals. Use ewg.org to help you. We also have to evaluate what we clean with. For example, an easy, affordable, and effective household cleaner is white vinegar. You can do one part vinegar and two parts water and add a few drops of essential oil. This makes a great surface cleaner for anywhere in the house, even the bathroom and kitchen. You can clean toilets with white vinegar and a little bit of dish soap. You can also clean floors with a steam mop, or if you clean them by hand, use one part vinegar to two parts water and a drop of dish soap.

Relationships

Continue having sit-down meetings with your family, or do your meeting while you're prepping food! A weekly check-in is ideal. This will help keep everyone accountable to the tasks that they are supposed to be doing for their own health and as a contribution to the home and family.

Mom and Dad need their own time, and so do other caretakers. Start planning a date night once a month. Make sure you are giving each other some time in the morning or before bed to talk and spend quality time together. It can be fifteen to twenty minutes. Just having that little time at the beginning or end of the day fosters connectedness and growth in a relationship. If you are a single parent, your alone or social time is important for your health. Find a good babysitter, and make time for yourself or to be with others.

Maybe there's a desire for more time with friends outside of the family. This is something that can be brought up at the weekly family meeting. If there is a painting night, a concert, dinner, or a show that Mom or Dad want to go see with their friends, keep the communication open and make everyone aware. Find a sitter if needed. Get it on the calendar. Communication is one of the biggest reasons why couples and families disagree or lose connectedness. We make too many assumptions. More direct communication is needed.

Work-Life Balance

And just as we need interaction, we also need to create boundaries for rest and downtime. Too often, my clients are over-committed. There are many reasons for this. It could be overextension at work, people-pleasing, fear of being left out, or just being addicted to a higher-pace lifestyle. No matter what, your body, mind, and spirit need rest. Be more particular about where your energy and time are going because you never get it back. If you are currently in a work situation that is too demanding, this is something that needs attention as well. When work overwhelms other aspects of our life and who we are, then dis-ease is created.

Next Steps

Whole health can be achieved this year and beyond through reflecting on what God tells us, being honest about what we need, building a support system, and planning for success. From there, it's a matter of following straightforward, holistic principles for our primary foods, physical foods, and personal care practices to ensure health and well-being.

As you embark on this journey, I pray that you see you have everything you need to thrive and be well. Tune out the noise, and bring your focus to what is true and good. God bless you, and may you find health, happiness, and peace in the new year and beyond!

Chapter 7

When The Dark Night Lingers: Waking Up From Disillusion to Steadfast Hope

By Melissa Manion

"I REMAINED, LOST IN OBLIVION, MY FACE I RECLINED ON THE BELOVED, ALL CEASED AND I ABANDONED MYSELF, LEAVING MY CARES FORGOTTEN AMONG THE LILIES."
—ST. JOHN OF THE CROSS[18]

For some people, there is a single event or trauma that happens in their lives that changes the trajectory of everything. For others, there have been so many of those that we have not only lost count but also lost our way. We find ourselves sitting on the floor, looking around at the rubble of our lives, wondering, "How did I get here?" And asking, "Where are you, God?" We look back over the years, tracing our steps and poring over pages of written-down prayers. We see the times when the mental or physical pain didn't end, the relationship wasn't restored, the lines weren't there, or they were, but the baby was lost. The addiction still held its grip, the child still hadn't come home, the career was lost, or the life of someone you loved ended too soon.

---

[18] St. John of the Cross. "Dark Night of the Soul." *The Dark Night*, 1577-1579.

A Peaceful New Year

Oftentimes, these trials are interspersed with beautiful things. There are lives that are saved, miraculous interventions, apologies, and amends that we never expected. Community showing up without being asked or new friendships making the load more bearable. The suffering, in some way, has not been in vain. However, our hearts feel heavy and sick. The perseverance seems more like a constant pursuit of something elusive. Without our conscious awareness, we allow our disappointments to become our reality. Despair seeps in. The internal questioning becomes relentless. Disillusionment becomes our stalemate.

This is what some call the Dark Night of the Soul. Originally coined from a poem written by St. John of the Cross, it has come to represent finding ourselves in a desert wasteland type of place in our faith. We have endured so many painful seasons that we have almost altogether lost our faith. I know because I've been there. I found myself questioning everything I thought I knew about God. It was an unraveling of sorts. Painful but necessary. You see, when I got to the end of my tangled-up rope, what I found was that through all of my trials and tribulations, the only person I truly could control was me. On the surface, this may seem helpful, and to a certain degree, it was. However, what had crept in unsuspectingly was also a belief that "I" was the only one in control.

It was Autumn 2021 when my family and I all fell sick with that nasty virus that caused the world to shut down. Thankfully, I was the only one to suffer greatly. I found myself unable to sleep or eat, losing 30 pounds I didn't have to lose. In and of itself, the situation was awful. Simultaneously, my father had fallen incredibly ill and was hospitalized for almost a month. It truly looked as though he wasn't going to make it. I then got a call from my mom telling me that after nearly 17 years in remission, she had breast cancer again. This time a double mastectomy was the only option. She had not been in good health for most of my life, so reasonably, I was concerned. My emotions were raging like a storm at sea because, aside from all these things coming to a head at once, I was buckling under the weight of years of running from my pain. Traumas started early in my life, and they were unrelenting. I was exposed to things and situations no child should endure. I fell victim to sexual assault, suffered the traumatic loss of a child through abortion, and walked through life-altering situations with my oldest children. In addition to the excruciating pain of having my sister ripped from my life, I lost my brother to a car accident and a best friend to suicide. Then, there were years of debilitating chronic pain that would yield and return at will. Yet, I just kept on pushing forward. Telling myself it would be ok. Convincing myself that I was fine, my children would be fine, my unsteady marriage would work out okay. If only I could just do this or that, I could keep it all afloat.

So, in the midst of being incredibly sick, both my parents' health and lives hanging in the balance, and trying to keep my head above water at home with a struggling marriage and two young daughters who desperately needed me...I broke. Quite literally. Something happened inside my brain that caused everything to go haywire. I had seen movies where people had mental breakdowns, but I had never experienced one in real life. It was as if a switch was flipped, and everything went offline. From October through January,

I was a shell of myself. I began having multiple panic attacks a day. I would pace around my block gasping for air, crying out to the LORD to "Please help me." Every minute was an attempt at survival. Fear became my primary emotion. Sleep evaded me, and living felt like dying slowly. I was trapped inside my breaking-down body, and no matter how hard I tried, nothing I did could free me from the prison inside my own head. I could truly see no end, no way out. I have a vivid memory of my husband and I driving in our truck one afternoon, and I said to him, "I don't think I'm going to make it through this," to which he replied, "Of course you are! You've got this." The look on my face let him know the level of desperation and despair I was in. I wasn't merely suggesting that this breakdown wouldn't end but rather that I didn't know if I would be able to endure it.

This was where the LORD met me and began to change me to my core. I like to say He showed up right there in the middle of my broken-down mess, but really, He had been there all along. I am sharing with you because I know I am not alone. Maybe (by God's grace), you haven't had a mental breakdown, and I truly hope that by heeding my words, you can head that off at the pass. As I said, this didn't happen overnight. It was a slow and steady erosion. In fact, it was the result of years and years of trauma after trauma, heartbreaks, and heartaches that I tried in my own strength to overcome. It was unacknowledged pain covered up by an abundance of head-knowledge faith. Which I assure you is a dangerous combination. The most important piece of all of this was that it wasn't as if God hadn't shown up. It was more that I couldn't remember that He did.

On 10/10/21, I wrote in my journal, "I am realizing that since I have conditioned myself to believe that the only person I can control is me, I have also believed that I am the only person in control! This extends to you, Lord. I am afraid that if I trust in you and a number of things don't change or improve, it will cause me to doubt your willingness or even ability to help me. So if I just leave room for doubt or for lowering my expectations of you, as I attempt to do with some of the people in my life, then you won't hurt me or let me down as many others have. Which then leaves ME striving to control. Which is futile and painful. Lord—I believe, help my unbelief."

Some of you reading this are at the beginning of a new year and are feeling full of zest and zeal, making all kinds of resolutions and expecting greatness. I think that is amazing, truly I do. I also believe you should read on. Sometimes, all the planning and doing are the very things that God will ask you to let go of. In a general sense, organization and structure are incredibly important. When God set the world into motion, He brought beauty from nothing. His Word assures us He is a God of order and structure, not of chaos and disarray. So, by all means, write the lists and set the goals!

Having said that, if you find yourself where I did, not only in January of 2022 but many Januarys before, wondering how you could possibly have any hope left in your body, mind, or soul, I'm so glad you found me here. I trust that you are reading this at just the right time. Jesus was very clear when He spoke to us in John 16:33, saying, "I have told you these things, so that in me you will have peace. In this world you will have trouble. But take heart! I have overcome the world."

Yes friend, take heart. You are not alone in the wrestling and pain! There is hope, I promise. It's just not going to be found in all your best-laid plans. Hope and healing is found in your belief, and I am here to challenge you on exactly what it is that you are believing.

To begin, let's dive into the Word. In Mark chapter 9, verses 14-29, we find the story of a grieving father. If you are not familiar, I'll share that it says he has "brought his son, who is possessed by a spirit that has robbed him of his speech." The man tells Jesus, "I asked your disciples to drive out the spirit, but they could not." Jesus replies, "You unbelieving generation..." The father pleads with Jesus, "But if you can do anything, take pity on us and help us." Jesus immediately responds with a very important question and statement: "'If you can?' said Jesus, 'Everything is possible for one who believes.'"

My first challenge to you is this: when you look at your struggles or look back on the collective years of trials, what questions do you have regarding how Jesus LOVES you? Do you wonder if you are even worthy of that love at all? Maybe you question if you are even worth having pity on. In order to have pity for someone, you would need to have sympathy and compassion for them and their situation. If we have found ourselves time and time again wondering why God seems so indifferent about our pain, we may very well question the love He has for us.

But don't miss this...the grieving father SHOWED UP to Jesus with his son.

Let's now find ourselves in the book of Mark, chapter 5, verses 25-34. Here, we come across the story of the bleeding woman, in pain and given no name. We read of how she "had been subject to bleeding for twelve years. She had suffered a great deal under the care of many doctors and had spent all she had, yet instead of getting better, she only grew worse. When she heard about Jesus, she came up behind him in the crowd and touched his cloak because she thought, "If I just touch his clothes, I will be healed."

My second challenge is this: how long have you been doubting if God really REDEEMS? Have you in all the striving and working to fix the things, forgotten Who actually has the power? How many plans have you made, and people have you sought out to mitigate the pain and suffering? Have you found yourself thinking, "If only I..." or "Why didn't I just..." If the pain still lingers and the weight hasn't been lifted, we may very well question the authority God has over our life. Or the willingness He has to intervene.

But don't miss this...despite her pain and suffering and the unspoken shame, she SHOWED UP bleeding at the feet of Jesus.

Now, let's take a look at Hagar. Her story in Genesis 16 is so special to me, not only because of how God met her in a literal desert place but also because she ascribes to God a significant name! A name so powerful it helps us catch our breath when the waves are overcoming us. Hagar is introduced to us in Genesis 16. We're told she is an Egyptian slave of Abram and Sarai. As the story unfolds, Sarai is growing impatient, waiting on the promise given to Abram from God that she would become pregnant and that he would be a father to many. "So she said to Abram, The LORD has kept me from having children. Go sleep with my slave; perhaps

I can build a family through her" (verse 2). The story goes on to tell us how Abram listens to his wife's request, sleeps with Hagar, and conceives a child. As one could imagine, this plan is not all rainbows and butterflies. We learn that Hagar's feelings towards Sarai begin to sour, and Sarai lashes out at Abram. Abram responds, saying, "Your slave is in your hands. Do with her whatever you think best." Then, the story goes on to say that "Sarai mistreated Hagar; so she fled from her" (verse 6). Hagar finds herself in the desert, likely questioning how she got to this point. I imagine her lamenting to herself at the terrible position she is now in. It's at that moment an angel of the LORD comes to her and speaks to her weary heart. This is where we are told: "She gave this name to the LORD who spoke to her: You are the God who sees me. For she said, I have now seen the One who sees me" (verse 13). El Roi—the God who sees me.

My third challenge is this, have you been through so much that you look around and see nothing but wasteland? Do you wonder if God even SEES you? Have you wondered if the paths you traveled have led you out of His sight? Is there even a way back?

But don't miss this...despite the disarray, she still SHOWED UP to hear the voice of the LORD and follow the guidance.

Are you catching the theme? None of these situations were under their control. Sure, we could pick apart all the ways that they could have or should have done things differently. Often that is how we live. Without even noticing, we take the wheel of not just our lives but the lives of all those around us that we love. We think and strategize and even sometimes conspire. Our best laid plans and well-meaning intentions become an idol without us even knowing it. Out of a desire for safety and comfort we sacrifice our faith on the altar of control and before we know it we are falling apart at the seams. We find ourselves quite literally sick and tired and struggling to hold on to any semblance of faith or hope. What we often fail to recognize is that the answer to our struggle isn't found in controlling the conditions but rather in recognizing and submitting to the One who actually is in control!

Please hear me, there is no quick fix or easy three-step process to come out of the darkness and into the light. However, it is absolutely possible and dare I say essential that you SHOW UP and BELIEVE.

There is a story in 2 Kings of a Shunammite woman who insists that her husband make a room for Elisha in their home. Elisha comes to her home, takes her up on her hospitality and noting her generosity and belief in his righteousness prophesied that she would be with child. This was her greatest desire. Her son is born and grows until one day he says to his father, "My head. My head" (4:19). The boy is then taken to the arms of his mother, where he dies. The mother says she will go and see Elisha, a man of God, and come back. Her final words to her husband upon departure were: "It will be alright" (4:26).

> Do you believe it will be alright?
> Do you believe God loves you?
> Do you believe God redeems?
> Do you believe God sees you?

What do you believe? Grab a pen and paper and ask God to show you. Ask Him where fear has come in. Ask him where doubt has taken hold. Ask Him what lies you are believing and then ask what truth needs to replace it and be written on your heart. Write down what you hear and speak it over yourself! Day after day until it becomes the truth you hold dear.

I deeply believe that light shines in the darkness and that the darkness has not, cannot and will not overcome it. I also believe that in order for that to be true we must bring what we keep hidden in the darkness into the light! Most of us will struggle to admit or acknowledge that we are striving for control. It is often not until we have broken down physically, spiritually and mentally that we can even begin to see that we need to let go. It is even harder to admit and find a space where we can acknowledge that a lack of belief or a questioning of faith have become the result of the dark night of the soul lingering too long.

So let's pretend we are sitting across the table in a quaint little coffee shop, caramel macchiato in hand. I want you to know that I've come to give you permission to ask these questions and wrestle with the answers. I'm looking you in the eyes and encouraging you that against all odds, you can find the faith to believe. I want to tell you that you are loved and seen and valued, not just by me (and likely many others) but most importantly by the GOD who created the universe and knew you in your mother's womb! I am giving you a hug and permission to cry and to grieve and to let go and begin again. Borrow my belief that God "is able to do immeasurably more than all we ask or imagine according to his power that is at work within us" (Ephesians 3:20). One day at a time, choose to have faith not in yourself or your abilities, but in God who loves you more than you know. Pray, "I believe, help my unbelief." Know that it is ok to live in what I like to call the "both, and."

    You can be in pain *and* have hope.
    You can lament your circumstances *and* have joy.
    You can question where God is *and* trust that he is there.
    You can be honest about your doubts *and* still have belief.

As you set off on this new year with lists and resolutions in mind, would you put down the planner for just a moment and whisper something important to God? Would you whisper the prayer I had written down in my journal just before my breakdown came? I am inviting you to do this because, little did I know, everything was about to fall apart so it could be put back together securely. Little did I know that I was about to let go of all my self-reliance and learn to truly let God in. Little did I know that love and peace would come rushing in too. Little did I know that I could never be enough, but that He always could. Little did I know that all my best laid plans could never compare to the Hope set before me. And I want that Hope for you too.

"Thank you Father, for seeing me, for loving me, for choosing me, for saving me. For Your patience, mercy and grace.

You alone are God. Holy, immeasurable. Good. All knowing. Loving Father. Help me to know You more. Help me to see You in all things. I want to be close to You, LORD.

Forgive me for the distance. You have always been right there. Remind me of who You are. Teach me who You are.

I believe, help my unbelief."

A *handful of my favorite verses to help you remember*:

Isaiah 54:10
Joshua 1:9
Psalm 4:8
Psalm 27:13
Philippians 4:4-9
Galatians 6:9
Matthew 11:28-30
John 14:27
Romans 8:24-25
2 Corinthians 12:9
2 Corinthians 1:3-4

Chapter 8

Moving from Perplexed to Purposeful: Focusing on God's Plan

By Nancy Radloff

> "FOR IT IS BY GRACE YOU HAVE BEEN SAVED, THROUGH FAITH—AND THIS IS NOT FROM YOURSELVES, IT IS THE GIFT OF GOD—NOT BY WORKS, SO THAT NO ONE CAN BOAST. FOR WE ARE GOD'S HANDIWORK, CREATED IN CHRIST JESUS TO DO GOOD WORKS, WHICH GOD PREPARED IN ADVANCE FOR US TO DO."
> —EPHESIANS 2:8-10

Happy New Year! The flip of the calendar gives us a fresh start and time to reflect on what's next. Life is not static. Transitions are inevitable. Some are planned, while others are unplanned. Life's circumstances ebb and flow.

Many times throughout my life, I stood at a crossroads, pondering just how to proceed. You, my friend, have been there too. Birthdays, transitions, decisions, unexpected job losses, financial strains, medical diagnoses, waiting on results, relationship difficulties, childcare complexities, memory care stress, an empty nest, retirement, trying not to worry, Covid's shutdown, praying for the best! Questions needed answers. Problems needed solutions.

I remember a time of perplexity while lying flat on my back in a dark recovery room after an invasive surgery. The only light was a night light. The instructions were to be still and not move. There were so many unknowns. There was so much beyond my control. Waiting was hard, really hard.

My mind went back to my mother's words, "Nancy Lynn, count your blessings." And so I did. I counted my blessings from God. My prayers moved from thankfulness to quiet tears streaming down my face, wondering what would be next, medically and personally. The diagnosis was not good.

IF this was it, how would I be remembered? What really mattered? The current situation would change when leaving the hospital. The surrounding circumstances would change depending on the diagnosis. We'd have a new normal, but how much time would we have together?

Then it hit me, in the stillness of my being, in the presence of God, that I was HIS from the beginning until now and forevermore. He who changest not abides with me! When everything else was stripped away, what really mattered was God's grace. Yes, Ephesians 2:8-9 resounded with God's gift of grace.

Songs of "worth-ship" filled my soul. My soul soared in the "worth-ship of God." My heart prayed for His will and for help to follow through with whatever would come to pass. Prayers for God's will in my re-purposement shifted from what I wanted to what God wanted for me.

Perplexed

At times, we all experience being perplexed. Different ages and stages of our lifespan present distinct challenges and choices. Perplexity in the child's space becomes a world of inquisitiveness and curiosity. Perplexity in the young adult's world often centers on self-awareness and impactful choices. Parents' perplexities pertain to the responsibilities and loving interests of their children and family life. Those retirees living in their empty nests face the challenges of all of the above.

This new year, how are your perplexities pushing in on you? Broken relationships? Building relationships? Medical issues? What are you seeking? A curiosity to learn new things? Impactful choices (career or lack of career)? Family responsibilities and the loving interest of your family? Some of the above? All of the above?

Being stuck in the hospital, not knowing what was next, created stress. My mind wandered, and my soul cried out to God. You probably have had those immobilizing times of being stuck, waiting, wondering what was going to happen. Disappointment, discontent, diagnosis, disaster, and decisions weighed heavily on your mind. Your transitions and life changes, planned or unexpected, created stress.

How have your perplexities in life overshadowed your purpose? Sometimes, surrounding circumstances press in so tightly, and current situations weigh so heavily that we cannot think clearly. Confusion constricts clarity of purpose.

It is during those perplexing moments that you and I can reflect and redirect our perspective. We can pivot to prayer and praise. We can "worth-ship" God—who from all things came and for whom we live (1 Corinthians 8:6). Moving from perplexed... starts with God's plan.

God's Plan

Who is God? He is the omnipotent Creator, the loving Redeemer, and the empowering Holy Spirit. When I pause to ponder God's greatness, my heart aligns with His eternal perspective. Remembering God's miracles and promises in His Word redirects my focus to God's omnipotence, omniscience, and omnipresence.

My mom was so wise. Counting blessings does shift the mindset to acknowledge God's faithfulness and His compassionate heart for His children.

Laying in post-op, embracing God's presence, Romans 8:28 came to mind, "And we know that God causes all things to work together for good to those who love God, to those who are called according to His purpose" (NASB). It was and still is such a comfort knowing that He who changest not is actively working in all things for me and for you!

Did you catch it? God is working for our good, according to His purpose. How can this be with all of the changes and uncertainties in life?

Go back, way back to the beginning. "In the beginning God created the heavens and the earth" (Genesis 1:1). Our omnipotent, all-powerful God created everything perfectly. God the Father was there creating the universe (Genesis 1:1). God the Holy Spirit was there hovering over the water (Genesis 1:2), and God the Son, Jesus, was there as the Word, and through Him all things were made (John 1:1-3).

God's plan of creation was to create a perfect world and abide with His children. Then God's first children, Adam and Eve, sinned. They blew it. They sinned. They disobeyed Almighty God. Perfection was gone. Sin and the negative effects of sin were now embedded in God's creation. From that moment on, all of mankind would be imperfect, needing restoration.

But wait, God still had a plan.

God's plan of redemption was given as early as Genesis 3:15, "And I [God] will make enemies Of you [Satan] and the woman, And of your offspring and her Descendant; He [Jesus] shall bruise you [Satan] on the head, And you shall bruise Him on the heel" (NASB). God promised a Savior.

Wow! God's plan included His forgiveness, redemption, and restoration of His fallen children. God's promise in Genesis 3:15 was fulfilled in John 3:16, "For God so loved the world, that He gave His only Son, so that everyone who believes in Him will not perish, but have eternal life" (NASB). Here, God reminds us of His loving plan to bring His people back into relationship with Him. God promised it, and God fulfilled it.

We, too, are part of God's plan and have been called according to His purpose. God created us. We are wonderfully made (Psalm 139:14). We are not here by accident. God created me, and God created you on purpose!

The age-old question of "Who am I?" is answered in 1 Peter 2:9, "But you are a chosen people, a royal priesthood, a holy nation, a people for God's own possession, so that you may proclaim the excellencies of Him who has called you out of darkness into His marvelous light" (NASB).

Created by God, your true identity is found in Him as a child of God. Write out 1 John 3:1 and post it on your bathroom mirror, "See how great a love the Father has given us, that we would be called children of God; and *in fact* we are. For this reason the world does not know us; because it did not know Him." What a wonderful affirmation!

Like Adam and Eve—when we blow it—when our sin separates us from God, our loving Father in heaven wants restoration. So God sent His Son Jesus to suffer crucifixion, die, and rise again as the required atonement for our sin. Jesus, the Lamb of God who takes away the sin of the world (John 1:29), restored our at-one-ment with God so that we could be in a right relationship with Him.

Redeemed by God, your value is in Christ's love for you. God took care of this. God made you once. He redeemed you back. Christ paid your redemption price.

Reread Ephesians 2:8, "For it is by grace you have been saved, through faith...." God's GRACE—God's Riches At Christ's Expense—saves your soul. What a relief!

Being created and redeemed are not our own doing. We can't do it. "No one can boast," declares the apostle Paul in Ephesians 2:9. God's work of salvation is by Christ alone. "Salvation is found in no one else, for there is no other name under heaven given to mankind by which we must be saved" (Acts 4:12). What a wonderful truth!

Back in the hospital, I called upon His name. Again and again, I was reminded that God's love and forgiveness are available to all who call on His name (Romans 10:13).

As the doctor explained my dire diagnosis and an unknown prognosis, believing in God's promises gave me a peace that passed my understanding. I clung to knowing that whether I lived or died, I belonged to the Lord (Romans 14:8). From my beginning until now, and forevermore, I am a redeemed child of God.

God wasn't abandoning me, and God doesn't leave you stranded here either. God is with us. As Jesus ascended back to heaven, He promised, "...I am with you always, to the very end of the age" (Matthew 28:20). God is omnipresent. He is always with you, with me—24/7.

God's love determines your self-worth. Your worth is not based on an accumulation of money or achievements. You are a child of God. You are important to God. You are redeemed by God. You belong to God. Taking this to heart can comfort you as you start this new year and during your times of confusion, stress, and distress.

Purpose Fulfilled through GTAs

God's plan determines your purpose for Him. Are you affirmed in your calling? Or are you searching for something more?

This generation, this season of life, this new year, this moment in time are exactly where God intended for you to be. As a child of God, God has a plan and a purpose for your life and for my life too. His Holy Spirit constantly equips us with all that we need to know and to do His will in whatever season of life we are living.

BUT what does God's purpose look like in our lives? What is our reason for being here? Simply stated, we are here to love God and love others for Him.

Ephesians 2:10 explains this, "For we are God's handiwork, created in Christ Jesus to do good works, which God prepared in advance for us to do." God's plan for us continues with His omniscience (full knowledge) and advance preparation for us to do good. God's got this all figured out!

Empowered by God, your purpose is planned by Him, for Him. Saved to serve, you and I are uniquely designed to be a blessing to others.

You may have heard of the phrase "time, treasure, and talents" when referring to applying God-given blessings for work in God's kingdom. These 3Ts of stewardship, while motivating for some, may become somewhat of a stumbling block for others.

What if I don't have the time? What if I don't have the treasure of money? What if I don't have a specialized talent? Some people may feel unqualified to serve. As a youth, I did not feel like I was enough. My heart wanted to serve. My mind was stuck in miserable, measurable comparisons to others. My dad kept reminding me, "Just be kind, always." Little did I know then that I would eventually grow into what God intended.

Reflect on that old adage of "time, treasure, and talents." Instead of thinking, "We have to be qualified to serve God," here is a twist: Think of how you have already been blessed by God in big and small ways. These blessings already received are your GTAs—Gifts, Time, and Abilities—for living a purpose-filled life.

G—GIFTS
Our GTAs include the concept of G–Gifts as blessings.

While the English language carries multiple meanings of individual words, the word *gift* can serve us well. It can be thought of in a variety of ways. The most obvious gift is the wrapped present given and received on a birthday or at Christmas. You probably open these gifts with joy.

A broader use of the term *gift* brings to mind the blessings we have received from God. These blessings are both spiritual and material. The most lavish gift given by God is His love in sending Jesus to be our Savior from sin (John 3:16-17, Ephesians 2:8-9). Our gift of faith is of eternal value.

Galatians 5:22-23 lists nine intangible gifts from the Holy Spirit: love, joy, peace, patience, kindness, goodness, faithfulness, gentleness, and self-control. Keep your fruits of the Spirit in mind as you put your GTAs to use.

The first material blessing that comes to mind when thinking about our "treasure" is money. Using the word "Gift" in defining GTAs encompasses *more* than money. Our GTAs include those gifts of financial blessing and other resources to share. You may have been financially blessed, or you may have been blessed with alternative resources, including clothing, shoes, home goods, furniture, or supplies to donate. If you are a business owner, sharing your WIFI connections with guests becomes a blessing in disguise. Perhaps you have physical building space for other people to utilize. Keeping small "Blessing Bags" in your car provides comfort for others as needed.

God has blessed us with a variety of gifts to use in support of others in need. Pause to pray. List your tangible and intangible gifts.

T–TIME

Our GTAs include the concept of T-Time as a blessing.

We each have been given the same 24 hours, 7 days a week. How we spend our time is a choice! Someone feeling a time crunch declares, "I just don't have the time." Someone else may look at Psalm 118:24 and proclaim, "This is the day that the LORD has made; let us rejoice and be glad in it!" God gives us time. What about your days?

Whether you feel that you have available time or a lack of time, look at your calendar for the new year. It organizes your monthly events and weekly schedules. Think about those blocks of time that you have already planned. Inside these blocks are opportunities to be a blessing to others. Using your fruits of the Spirit, consider how you can serve others within that time frame. Look again. Do you have open time to spare in volunteering or helping others? Intentionally plan unspoken acts of kindness to family, friends, coworkers, or others in those little bits of time that pop up.

Time engages people in different ways throughout life. Blocks and bits of time look differently for busy parents, diligent community workers, dedicated college scholars, developing entrepreneurs, or retired folks with time to spare while looking for re-purposement. Each person lives out a rhythm of life in varied beats and measures of time.

God blesses each of us with a lifetime lived out in moments. Some people will have more time here on Earth than others. This is your time. God created you for a time such as this. Pause to pray. List your blocks and bits of time.

A—ABILITIES

Our GTAs include the concept of A–Abilities as blessings.

God equips each of us with something to use for Him! Envision the concept of abilities as not only a developed talent or skill but also as an area of interest to pursue. Consider what makes you unique. What are your hobbies? Do you have a specific talent or skill? These areas of interest can be utilized in God's service for the good of others and to His praise.

God assures us that while different GTAs are assigned, it is the same God who plans and provides them all. "There are different kinds of gifts [GTAs], but the same Spirit distributes them. There are different kinds of service [interests and skills], but the same Lord. There are different kinds of working [helping], but in all of them and in everyone it is the same God at work" (1 Corinthians 12:4-6).

The Holy Spirit works faith in our hearts and equips us with what we need to know and to do His will, according to His plan and purpose. You are blessed to be a blessing! Pause to pray. List your areas of interests and skills as abilities.

Orbits as Opportunities

Our GTAs include the concept of orbits as opportunities.

Now that you have identified your GTAs, how will you respond? Whom will you serve?

Think of the people in your life—family, friends, coworkers, church members, teams, volunteer circles, and community groups. These connections are your orbits. Some of these relationships and connections are closer than others.

Jesus teaches us to prioritize our orbits in His Great Commission (See Acts 1:8). God sent His own disciples to go out and work for Him, starting with reaching those people closest to home.

Our orbits will vary. My orbits will provide a certain outreach. Your orbits will reach different people. God's Word reminds us that "Each of you should use whatever gift [GTAs] you have received to serve others [orbits], as faithful stewards of God's grace in its various forms" (1 Peter 4:10).

Draw your orbits as concentric circles with Christ's cross in the center. Next, write the names of people and organizations important to you in their circles. Consider how you can help each one using your GTAs. Add your unique GTAs—Gifts, Time, and Abilities—to your circles of influence. This diagram can help you visualize your customized plan of action.

Personal orbits are opportunities for you to help and encourage individuals in your life. Pause to pray. List your orbits and opportunities to be of service.

***

My diagnosis determined my medical journey and adaptations in my new normal. The landscape of life changed a bit, but my identity as God's child remained anchored in who God is and in what He has done as Creator, Redeemer, and Sanctifier. God's plan didn't end there. His purposes continue.

God has a plan and a purpose for you too! Motivated by God's love for us, we can make use of our God-given GTAs and Holy Spirit-driven orbits as opportunities to provide support and service to others. "We love, because He first loved us!" (1 John 4:19, NASB).

"Finally, brothers and sisters, whatever is true, whatever is noble, whatever is right, whatever is pure, whatever is lovely, whatever is admirable—if anything is excellent or praiseworthy—think about such things." —Philippians 4:8

Next Steps... Take time for reflection on your GTAs and orbits!
    Reflect on the poem below, filling in your uniqueness or favorite Holy Scriptures.
    Review your GTAs and orbits by listing them.
    Recommit your heart to God's purposes.
    Reflect on the poem, filling in your uniqueness or favorite Holy Scriptures.

Perplexed to Purpose
by Nancy Radloff

Pondering _____

Problems _____

Pivot _____

Perspective _____

To Praise _____

With God's Plans _____

Purposeful Plan-of-Action _____

A Paradigm to Proceed! _____

Review your GTAs and orbits by listing them below.

G—GIFTS (Financial and Resources)

_____

T—TIME (Blocks and Bits)

_____

A—ABILITIES (Areas of Interest and Skill)

_____

Orbits (Circles of Opportunities)

_____

Recommit your heart to God's purposes.
> **Dear God, Thank you...**
> for creating me as Your masterpiece,
> for redeeming me through Jesus' salvation, and
> for empowering me to serve others in ways that You have planned.
> Thank You for blessing me with the gifts, time, abilities, and opportunities needed to be a blessing to others. Inspire my heart and direct my days. In Jesus' name. Amen and Alleluia!

Chapter 9

Grounded in Grace: How to Set Grace-Filled Goals When Life Happens

By Jess Henning

"NOW TO HIM WHO IS ABLE TO DO FAR MORE ABUNDANTLY THAN ALL THAT WE ASK OR THINK, ACCORDING TO THE POWER AT WORK WITHIN US, TO HIM BE GLORY IN THE CHURCH AND IN CHRIST JESUS THROUGHOUT ALL GENERATIONS, FOREVER AND EVER. AMEN."

—EPHESIANS 3:20-21 ESV

I paced anxiously across my bathroom floor. I turned away from the mirror; I couldn't look at myself. Burning tears filled my eyes. I couldn't believe it. Yet somehow, I knew it was true.

"Oh, my Lord." Those words were all I could manage to spit out. "Oh my! Lord. Oh, MY Lord!"

My hands trembled as I called my husband. The first time, it went to voicemail. When he finally answered the second time, his voice was soft, "Hey babe—what's up? I'm in a meeting."

I couldn't speak. The words wouldn't come. I began to

A Peaceful New Year

choke up as I drew in short and shallow breaths. I choked back the tears, and a strange cry came out. I sensed his concern as his tone quickly changed. "Are you okay? What's wrong?" It took every fiber in my being to utter the words to him.

My world felt as though it was spinning out of control. I didn't know what to do. I replayed what the nurse said to me over and over in my head. "Hundreds of millions of cells...ten weeks along."

In that one moment, I felt as though everything I had worked for—all my goals and carefully made plans—flew out the window.

Maybe you've found yourself in a similarly overwhelming situation. You see, *this* was not in our plans. In fact, my husband and I made careful plans to ensure this *wouldn't* happen.

We spent the past ten years of our marriage working to dig our way out of massive student loan debt. We weren't out of the woods yet. But we were finally gaining traction to make positive financial gains for our family of five.

We could nearly *taste* financial freedom! We'd planned carefully, thoughtfully, prayerfully.

* * *

I imagine you're probably like me, and you enjoy making plans and setting goals. It's fun to dream about what the future holds. It's exciting to write it down on paper—on purpose. Setting goals makes your dreams feel real.

When January rolls around each year, you do what every ambitious woman does: you create your goals. Big, *audacious* goals. (That is me, for sure!) Some of us call them resolutions, some of us have specific milestones we want to hit, and some of us even host elaborate get-togethers to create detailed vision boards (Yep, I've done that one too).

You're high on optimism, and you feel like nothing can stop you. There's nothing quite like that "new year, new me" energy—until life throws you a curveball.

The Reality of Setbacks

Imagine now it's mid-March. Suddenly, you're blindsided by an unexpected life event: a death in the family, a job loss, an unplanned pregnancy. Or maybe it's simply the slow accumulation of responsibilities, the things you didn't account for when you were mapping out your perfect year.

In a single moment, the goals you were so excited about feel like distant dreams. You feel overwhelmed, paralyzed by the sheer weight of it all, unsure of how to move forward.

And let's be honest—those setbacks? They're frustrating. Watching your goals slip through your fingers can make it feel as though your whole year is flatlining. You start to beat yourself up, questioning your ability, your purpose, and your worth. Why even set goals if life has a way of making them seem impossible to reach?

But what I've learned through my journey is that when I allowed myself to adjust and adapt, I didn't lose momentum—I gained clarity. I learned to trust the Lord with my plans and that sometimes a detour is exactly where I'm meant to be.

My pastor puts it this way: "Sometimes your setbacks are a setup for a comeback."

Why Create Goals at All?

I've been in the trenches. I've been the mom juggling a thousand things, feeling like my dreams were slipping through the cracks of my busy life. I've had those moments where I questioned everything—my ability, my purpose, and whether it was even worth continuing to set goals, or honestly, if I should just settle, thinking that this is "all there is" to life.

I get it, friend. But I want to remind you that your goals matter. They're so much more than things you simply want to achieve. They represent the path of where you want to go in life and, ultimately, the dreams of who you want to become and who God has called you to be.

Maybe you have a goal to become a six or seven-figure business owner. But your underlying motivation is that you want to have complete financial freedom so you can be generous towards others. (I'm raising my hand with you!)

Perhaps your goal is to lose 30 pounds. Not only because you want to live a longer, healthier life but because you know you'll look good—fitting into those skinny jeans again—which would make you feel confident and sexy.

Your goals are a powerful way to align your actions with your deeper desires and values. They serve as both a roadmap and a mirror—reflecting what truly matters to you and guiding you toward the person God has called you to become. Goals help you stay intentional, ensuring that each step you take leads you closer to your vision for the future.

Whether it's financial freedom, health or confidence, your goals provide the structure that turns abstract dreams into tangible results. They're not just about achievement.

They're about becoming, growing, and living in alignment with your purpose.

The Power of Grace

I believe in the power of setting goals. But I also believe in the power of grace. It's the difference between giving up and pressing on. It's what helps us thrive amid life's unpredictability.

In 2 Corinthians 12, Paul writes vulnerably about the thorn in his side. He was encouraged when the Lord told him, "My grace is sufficient for you, for my power is made perfect in weakness."

Grace gives you the strength to move forward.

You can choose to surrender your goals to God and allow grace to step in. Grace for yourself, grace for your plans, and grace for your changing circumstances. You know goal setting is important—it gives you direction, purpose, and motivation. But rigidly holding yourself to goals without acknowledging that "life happens" is setting yourself up for disappointment.

The truth is life *will* happen. Unexpected events will disrupt your plans. Instead of feeling defeated, what if you learned how to adapt your goals to fit your season? What if you allowed yourself the grace to modify, recalibrate, and move forward without feeling guilty about "not hitting your goal?"

It's time to redefine your relationship with goal setting. It's about giving yourself permission to create what I like to call "Grace-Filled Goals." These are goals that allow room for life's inevitable twists and turns. Goals that are not only achievable but adaptable.

Before you can set a grace-filled goal, you need to start with a mindset shift.

Long after you set this book down, the one thing I want you to take away from this chapter is this: **You can always choose to change your goals.**

You may be familiar with the saying, "The only thing constant in life is change." So, if you know your life will constantly experience change—why wouldn't you change your goals to align with where you are and the new direction you're going?

Just as you grow and change, your goals can change too. This powerful thought allows you to be open to the idea of changing your goal when your circumstances change. In times when your life feels out of control, this mindset shift helps you have a better sense of being in control.

Surrendering your goals to God and putting on this new mindset of choosing to change your goals is one of the most freeing experiences. It's time to say goodbye to feeling guilty over not hitting your goals!

Before you dive into the "hows" of setting grace-filled goals, consider the goals you've already made. Ask yourself: *Is this goal still aligned with my current reality?* When you ask this question, you are taking a purposeful step toward growth. If the answer is no, that's okay. It doesn't mean you've failed. It means you're growing. You're being responsive to life's shifting tides.

When you're ready to let go of all the ways you think your goals "should be," keep on reading.

Setting Grace-Filled Goals

So, what is a grace-filled goal? How do you create a goal filled with grace? How do you maintain progress while honoring the ebb and flow of life's circumstances?

A grace-filled goal honors both your ambition and your humanity. It's a goal set with intention but held with flexibility, allowing space for growth, setbacks, and life's unexpected turns.

A close friend recently shared her experience with setting goals. Anytime she didn't hit a goal, she felt like a failure. She always created high-pressure goals for herself. And she wasn't willing to compromise because compromising meant she wasn't doing a good enough job and that she should do better. All this negative self-talk left her no room for self-compassion. Have you had a similar experience when it comes to your goals?

Friend, it's time to stop "shoulding" all over yourself.

Unlike rigid, pressure-filled goals, grace-filled goals recognize that progress isn't always linear and that self-compassion is as important as the outcome itself. Grace-filled goals inspire you to move forward with purpose while embracing the imperfect journey of becoming who you're meant to be.

Create Goals Made for Your Journey

When I started my first business, I devoured every business book I could possibly read in my spare time. I didn't have a business degree, and I knew very little about running and marketing a business. As the saying goes, I didn't know what I didn't know. I earnestly sought wisdom and advice from others who'd been there. A book that influenced my thought process early on was Michael Hyatt's bestseller *Best Year Ever*.[19]

I learned not only how to set goals and implement the framework he taught—but even more powerful than that—I learned how to write my goals down. On paper. On purpose.

Hyatt shares five main reasons why it's important to write down your goals. First, it helps you get clear on what you want. Second, Hyatt says, "Writing down your goals helps you overcome resistance." Third, you are motivated to act on your goals. Fourth, your written goals act as a filter for what you want to say yes and no to. And finally, Hyatt writes, "It enables you to see—and celebrate—your progress."

Even in our digital age, studies have shown the power of writing things down. A study conducted by Dr. Gail Matthews of the Dominican University of California shows that you are up to 40 percent more likely to hit your goals if you write them down.[20] Forty percent! Who wouldn't want those odds?

You may be wondering if there's some magical tool, notebook, or planner that will help you reach your goals.

There are many goal-setting frameworks that exist, along with great systems and, yes, gorgeous paper planners,

---

[19] Hyatt, Michael. *Best Year Ever*. Baker Books, 2018.

[20] Matthews, Gail. "The Impact of Commitment, Accountability, and Written Goals on Goal Achievement." www.scholar.dominican.edu/psychology-faculty-conference-presentations/3/. Accessed 14 October 2024.

too. (I see you strolling through the stationery aisle in Target!) I invite you to try the daily goal planner I designed for creative entrepreneurs. Or you could use one of the seven pretty notebooks you picked up on your recent Target run or even a sticky note!

My best advice is to find a system that works for you and stick with it.

No matter what type of goal-setting framework or planner you decide on, it's important to write down your goals. Writing down your goals makes them tangible. It's a visual reminder of what you're working toward and the road map for where you're going in your individual journey.

Now, how do you turn regular goals into grace-filled goals?

When you write your goals down, plan to review them often. Once a month is good, but weekly or daily is even better. When your season changes, you rewrite and revise them! Writing your goals down doesn't mean they're written in stone. It also doesn't mean you're abandoning the goals you originally set.

Give yourself permission to update your goals when life happens. Revising your goals means you're allowing them to shift and transform with you as you grow. And when you update your goals, you can re-align them with your current season.

Let's dive deeper into how you can set grace-filled goals that align with your season.

Create Goals Made for Your Season

Years ago, a co-worker who'd become a good friend of mine and I created a lifestyle blog as a fun, creative outlet outside of our work. We got into a good rhythm of writing and posting regularly. We were having fun, and we also had dreams of turning the blog into something bigger for both of us.

Several years later, I was expecting my third son, working overtime, and traveling for a season every few weeks for my job. It was rough on my family, and we felt like we were running on a never-ending treadmill to keep up with our student loans.

The overwhelming demands of my young family and my work felt like too much. Something had to give. My heart was in the right place, but with the support of my friend, I decided the blog was no longer a fit for my season. I had to set it down. It was no longer a priority—my family, my health, and my work were all I could prioritize in that season.

It was a hard choice, but I knew it was the right one because I felt a great sense of peace after making that decision.

You may be facing some hard decisions too. You might need to make difficult choices about what you can pick up and what you need to set down in your current season.

When you define your season, you can create goals that are right for your season of life, which is transformational for both your personal life and your professional life.

Let's talk about some examples of different types of seasons—note that you may fall into several different seasons. Perhaps you are...

- A brand new mom with an infant
- Recently married, re-married, or divorced
- A new business owner or entrepreneur making a big shift in your business
- About to be an empty nester
- Retired/or starting a second career
- Caring for elderly parents
- Moving across the country to start a new job

Use the following questions as a guide to help you determine your season. Grab a notebook and pen. Take a moment to write down your current season in life.

- Are you in a season of high capacity, where you have the time, energy, and focus to tackle your biggest dreams?
- Are you in a season of growth, where you're building steady momentum, learning, and nurturing the foundations of your goals?
- Are you in a season of healing, where rest and reflection take priority?

As you consider your goals, you can also ask yourself, why is this a goal for me? Am I excited about this goal? Is this right for me right now in my season of life?

Let's be super clear here: the adjustments you make to your goals should reflect where you are—not where you think you *should* be.

One of my favorite business coaches and friend, Christy Wright, has told me, "Your season is simply *where* you are; it's not *who* you are."

Isn't that great news? You are *not* your season. It is *not* an identity marker. It's a location marker on the map of life.

Another way I've heard it: your season is determined by how much free time you have. I'd like to add, as a busy mom of boys, that your season is also determined by how much energy you have!

For example, in this season of my life with young kids, I will not create a goal that says, "I want to read 30 professional development books this year." Let's be real: most days, I barely have 30 seconds to myself, let alone the time to read a stack of books that's as tall as my preschooler. I know that's not right for me in my current season.

However, I do want to better myself through the power of reading, and I have a long list of titles accumulating on Goodreads. With all the crazy chaos in my house, sitting down to read is a rarity, so audiobooks have become my new bestie. I've built reading, or rather listening, into my daily routine to ensure I'm growing in this area of my life. This frees me from being stressed out about trying to hit a goal that is not a fit for my season.

When you identify your season by being honest and self-aware, you will create better goals that align with your priorities (aka, what matters most to you at this time in your life). Embrace your season so you can say 'yes' to the best things and 'no' to the things that aren't right for you right now.

Once you know your season, your priorities become clear, allowing you to create grace-filled goals that align with what matters to you most.

Create Goals Made for Your Priorities

Today, I met with my writer's group and caught up with them on things going on in my world, and honestly, it's all been things that feel big and overwhelming and some things that feel out of control.

I shared the anxiety I was feeling about the looming deadline for this very chapter I'm writing. Saying it out loud made me realize how unclear I was about what I needed to focus on right now.

One friend encouraged me by saying that even though I have so many things going on, if I know that this one project is ending soon, then why not take a few weeks to simply focus on completing my chapter?

The bigger challenges could wait. She pointed out that I would survive the next few weeks without making these huge life decisions. Thank goodness for friends who will speak truth into your life!

I needed to purposefully refocus my priorities.

This gave me permission to set aside my worries about all the other things on my plate to focus on what was most important that needed to be accomplished right now. Many of us, myself included, get stuck when we find ourselves confusing the urgent things in life for the important things.

Perhaps you can relate. Perhaps it feels like there are too many major decisions looming over you. Everything feels urgent, and it all needs to happen *right* now. My sweet friend, it doesn't. You are human, after all. You can't physically, emotionally, and mentally do it *all*. Certainly not all right *now*.

Christy Wright also writes about this in her bestselling book *Take Back Your Time*.[21] She writes, "Your time, money

---
[21] Wright, Christy. *Take Back Your Time.* Ramsey Press, 2021.

and energy are finite. You're always going to have to make choices. You can either make choices that reflect what matters most to you or you can try to do it all and fail."

I believe this matters because here's a hard truth I wish someone had told me—especially in my early years of juggling parenting and career life—this may not be your season to "get everything done."

Here's the good news—you can choose to make your goals fit your priorities. This is exactly where grace steps in.

Grace-filled goals aren't rigid; they're fluid. They move with you, not against you.

Considering your season, be purposeful about your priorities and ask, what and who do you want to spend your time on? What's right for you right now?

These things become your priority for right *now*.

Making Space for Grace

When I was expecting with our last kiddo, it was the first time I had to make my own maternity leave plan as an entrepreneur. How do you take time off after having a baby when you are both the boss *and* the workforce? It was a confusing time, and I felt like there were no clear answers.

Thankfully, with my husband's support and the wisdom of other women entrepreneurs who'd been there before, I created a plan that would work for me and my family. This helped me feel more confident going into this season when I wasn't sure what to expect.

If a major life event has left you feeling depleted, maybe it's time to shift from a goal that requires high output to one that encourages personal care and restoration. If family demands have ramped up, perhaps a career goal gets put on hold—but that doesn't mean it's abandoned. When life changes, you don't have to throw away your goals—you can revise them.

The questions listed below were the prompts I used to prepare for maternity leave when I felt completely unsure how to handle this unknown territory as an entrepreneur. They helped me to gather all my swirling thoughts and provided clarity so I could move forward.

Consider your season and your priorities and ask the following questions. Take your time to journal your thoughts on each. You can come back to these questions again and again, with every new season that comes your way. Mark this page right now so you can use these questions as a guide for future seasons.

- What things have held me back?
- What stresses me out? What things are going to stress me out in this season?
- What were things I said yes to and then dreaded? These are red flags to avoid.
- What leaves me exhausted?
- What things do I need to change?
- What is going to make me feel like I'm winning?
- What still feels right for my season? What do I want to say 'yes' to?
- What no longer serves me in this season? What do I want to say 'no' to?
- How can I adjust my goals to honor my current capacity and circumstances?
- Who do I need to reach out to for help?

Remember, grace-filled goals require flexibility, compassion, and self-awareness. They are a reminder that you're not a machine but a human being navigating the ups and downs of life.

But you might still be wondering: How can I extend grace to my goals in a practical sense?

Choosing Progress over Perfection

I'm a self-admitted recovering perfectionist. I could spend an hour editing one email. I could take an entire week to mull over the right phrasing for a blog post. I could take a month to make sure my social media content is planned out just right. Can you relate?

I've realized I'm amazing at starting new things: a new project, a fresh planner, an online course. You name it—if it's new, I'm there for it!

Finishing things, though? That's another story. Shocker, right? For years, I held a mental block that whatever I worked on couldn't possibly be done because it wasn't perfect yet. I felt grateful when I came across Jon Acuff's bestseller *Finish: Give Yourself the Gift of Done*.[22]

Acuff discusses the importance of overcoming the lie of perfectionism, writing, "This is the first lie that perfectionism tells you about goals: Quit if it isn't perfect." My mantra now for the past seven years has been, "Done is better than perfect." I tell myself that each time I don't feel ready to hit "post," "publish" or "send."

---

[22] Acuff, Jon. *Finish: Give Yourself the Gift of Done*. Penguin House, 2017.

Acuff shares three strategies I've applied to my goals, and you can use these practical tactics, too, when you find yourself in need of grace for your goals. The strategies are: extend your deadline, cut your goal, or combine.

Grace-Filled Strategy #1: Extend Your Deadline

I spoke at a business workshop this past summer, and a woman shared a huge goal she had for herself—by far one of the toughest and scariest goals out there, in my opinion. She was transitioning her side hustle to full-time so she could quit her 9-5 job that she didn't love. I could feel her passion but also the anxiety she must have felt over her goal as she spoke, saying she "had to do this" by the end of this year.

I sat back and listened as an Enneagram Type 2 would. When she paused, I waited a moment. Then, I asked her, "If you hit your goal in January or even February of the next year, how would that make you feel?" I loved her response when she smiled and said, "Well, that would still feel amazing!"

"It *would* feel amazing," I told her, "Because you still DID the thing!"

If you're worried about what will happen if you don't hit your deadline, take a moment and go down that road. Give an honest answer to "What is the worst thing that could happen if I don't get X done by Y?" I imagine it's not as terrible as you think.

Extend your deadline. More breathing space and a bit of room on your calendar will bring you peace in the process.

One small note on this: If you need to extend your deadline, I highly suggest you write this new deadline on your calendar. Don't extend your goal to "someday" or "maybe next year." It's important to give yourself an actual date to work toward. A grace-filled goal is still a goal, and that means it needs a deadline.

Grace-Filled Strategy #2: Cut Your Goal

One year for Christmas, I bought myself a book. I know, *glamorous.* But this was not just *any* book. It was Netflix's *Get Organized* co-founders Clea and Joanna's debut book, appropriately titled The Home Edit: A Guide to Organizing and Realizing Your House Goals.[23]

When the holiday chaos subsided for a moment, I cozied up on the couch with a blanket and my new book. I ran my fingers across the rich, semi-matte paper filled with gorgeous images of bathrooms, linen closets, and kitchen pantries all perfectly organized and styled in rainbow order, of course. As I slowly turned the pages, the words "Embracing the Low-Bar Lifestyle" caught my eye, causing me to pause and read.

I was intrigued. What was this magic they spoke of?

The way Clea and Joanna put it: "It's all about setting the bar just low enough that you can accomplish all kinds of bite-sized victories because life is too short for feeling residual guilt about not wearing real pants or making it to the gym *every* day."

On the surface, their Low-Bar Lifestyle seemed to be off-brand for The Home Edit team because everything they create is done with excellence. But as a busy mom, I *totally* get it.

---

[23] Shearer, Clea and Teplin, Joanna. *The Home Edit.* Clarkson Potter/Publishers, 2019.

Friend, make things easier for yourself—not harder!

We can apply the low-bar mentality to our goals, too, which aligns with Acuff's second strategy: Cut your goal in half.

Let's say you created a revenue goal for this year of $100,000. But because of changes in your season and shifts in your current circumstances, you need to adjust your goal. You can choose to cut your goal in half and set your new annual revenue target to $50k.

When you make $75k by the end of the year, you're feeling great about your accomplishment instead of feeling guilty.

I've heard from many women that they feel shameful for cutting their goal. It feels like you're cheating in life somehow by lowering the bar. Let's cut that lie out right now! There is no shame in adjusting your goals that will ultimately benefit you, your family, and your community. You can sensibly make changes to your goals without beating yourself up. You will be a more joyful wife, momma, boss, co-worker, and friend to those around you when you choose to set down the guilt and shame you've been carrying about your goals.

If you don't like the idea of cutting your goal by 50 percent, that's fine. Choose what percentage you want to cut your goal by. Need a little grace? Cut your goal by 10 percent. Need grace abundantly? Cut back 50 percent or more. The choice is yours.

At the end of the day, do what is best for you, your family and what you need in your season. No matter how much you choose to cut your goal by, there's always room for grace.

Embracing that low-bar lifestyle allows you to celebrate the small daily victories!

Grace-Filled Strategy #3: Combine Both Options

In January, I made a big goal to write 60,000 words to complete my first book's manuscript by June. I had planned everything down to the last detail and was determined to make it happen. Spring came, and as life would have it, the unexpected happened. I experienced major changes in my business and found myself going in a new direction. My big goal needed a big adjustment.

So, I made a tough but necessary decision: I cut my original word count goal in half *and* extended my deadline by six months. I realized I couldn't keep the same timeline and still give my family the attention they needed while I pursued a change in my business.

This wasn't my original vision, but it was the right fit for the season I was in. And the best part? It allowed me to still make progress toward my ultimate goal. I wrote, captured stories, jotted down ideas, and my creativity flowed better because the pressure was off. The experience taught me that sometimes, moving forward in smaller steps is exactly what you need to stay on track.

Everyone walks through difficult seasons. If you find yourself in one right now and need a little extra grace, remember that it's okay to blend strategies and adjust your goals to fit your reality. You get to decide what's right for you. Combining the first two options, cutting your goal, and extending your deadline may be the balance you need in your season.

Here's the deal: there is no "perfect" answer. Discovering the right balance does not happen overnight. I encourage you to try any combination of these grace-filled strategies and have patience for yourself in this process.

What's the key? Don't quit. Keep trying. Keep showing up, even if it means adapting along the way. Continue moving forward by refining your goal, which is grounded in both truth and grace simultaneously. Your goals are a journey, not a destination. The grace you offer yourself along the way will be your constant companion, gently encouraging you along the way, especially when things get tough.

Moving Forward With Grace

In 2017, I was let go from what was my first "real" job I got after college, which felt like a major setback. From there, I dove headfirst into entrepreneurship. In 2018, my goal was to match my former salary. With support from my network, word-of-mouth marketing, and by the grace of God, I hit my goal! In fact, I surpassed it. I felt confident going into the new year and created an even bigger revenue goal for 2019.

Spring came, and I woke up one cool April morning feeling like I could barely get out of bed. I dragged myself downstairs, only to plop back on the couch to lie down. Something was wrong. I felt dizzy, light-headed and sick to my stomach. "I must be coming down with the flu," I thought.

This went on, morning after morning, while my husband got our three boys ready for school. He urged me to go see my doctor. "Babe, you should get your bloodwork done. Something's obviously wrong!" He's sweet when he's worried about me. I think he was also weary from single parenting every morning.

I wanted answers, too.

Later that day, I went to my doctor's office. While there, the nurse asked me if I was pregnant. I literally laughed out loud and said, "Uh, nope. My husband had a vasectomy nearly two years ago!"

Pregnancy was not on my radar. It seemed like an impossible and silly question. I quickly put it out of my mind, having convinced myself I was dying from something else dramatically terrible.

That afternoon, as I waited in the carpool line to pick up child number two, I received a phone call from the nurse.

I nervously asked, "Well, what's wrong with me?" In a sweet Southern tone she said, "Honey, nothing's wrong with you. You're just 10 weeks pregnant."

The breath left my lungs. I nearly dropped my phone. "What?!" I asked in disbelief.

I zoned out as she continued to explain how my bloodwork showed there were hundreds of millions of cells present in my uterus. How on earth they can tell that from a blood sample is still mind-blowing to me.

Life happened, and it was truly a miracle. Clearly, God had other plans for my life.

When late fall of 2019 arrived, our curveball named Wesley was thrown into our lives, forever changing our family. Forever changing me.

In that defining moment of discovering an unexpected pregnancy, and in the weeks and months that followed,

I went on an unintentional journey of learning how to give myself and my big goals grace in that difficult season.

Throughout my pregnancy, I struggled. I cried. I grieved what felt like a loss of my dreams. But the Lord began working in me to guide me through the process. I slowly invited him in as I realized I couldn't get through that season on my own. Some days, it looked like sitting in uncomfortable silence. Grace was needed in proportion to the level of the unexpected interruption.

I may never understand God's timing in this life, but I am learning to embrace the great mystery of his ability to work within the messiness of life. I learned that there is always room for grace as you grow. I discovered that growth and grace aren't mutually exclusive; in fact, they go hand in hand.

My hope for you is that when life happens, you can purposefully apply grace to your own goals. As you pursue your dreams and navigate the unexpected, grace can be the very thing that fuels your growth rather than hinders it. Allowing yourself to evolve and adjust makes room for both ambition and self-compassion.

Remember—accepting grace is not a sign of weakness but a recognition of your strength—your strength to keep moving forward, even if it's in a new direction.

While the road ahead might not look like the one you originally mapped out, it doesn't mean you've lost your way. You're being led down a different path—and that path is filled with joyful possibilities you never could have asked for or imagined.

Choose to step into grace by creating grace-filled goals for your life. Give yourself permission to adapt, to rest, and to celebrate every step forward—even the small ones. When life shifts, let grace be your guide, reminding you that your journey doesn't have to be perfect to be purposeful.

I encourage you to embrace the beauty of progress over perfection and trust that your gracious heavenly Father will always meet you right where you are. My friend, take a deep breath, reset your intentions, and step boldly into the next chapter of your story—grounded in grace when life happens.

Chapter 10

Letting Go: Moving Forward Unburdened

By Stephanie Gavel

"COME TO ME, ALL YOU WHO ARE WEARY AND BURDENED, AND
I WILL GIVE YOU REST."
—MATTHEW 11:28

Humor me for a moment: imagine that you are sitting outside in your best-loved chair. The air is warm but with a slightly cool breeze. In hand, you have your favorite mug containing your favorite morning brew. A friend for years, I am sitting alongside you, and we are chatting away. Do you feel the warmth, the ease, and the comfort? After chatting for a few minutes, a comfortable pause occurs, and I ask you quietly: *how are things really going*? Does your breath hitch? Do you feel the tenseness come over you? Does your mind instantaneously struggle with *how much do I say*? Does that question make you swallow... hard? Do you allow your eyes to drift downward; do you avert your gaze before answering? Do you struggle with putting words to the burdens that you are carrying?

Even though we all long to live a life unencumbered, we get tripped up from time to time, entangled by past mistakes, words left unsaid, fears that are too weighty to be said aloud, and feelings that we struggle to fully identify. Sometimes, the battle we get caught up in is trying to figure out how we got here so that maybe we can fix it and make it right. But instead of being free, we remain stuck in that never-ending cycle.

I once saw this skit at a women's retreat. I can't remember much about the retreat, but I remember the skit. It was a portrayal of a woman, stooped over, dragging her burdens that no one else saw. Her gaze was cast downwards, her body was slumped, her gait slow and hesitant, and she often had to stop and rest. She kept those burdens gathered tightly to her body, making sure the chains that bound those things to her were tight, so much so that they became her self-imposed prison, blocking the road to freedom. She was so focused on holding onto those very things that were keeping her stuck, afraid that she would become exposed and that someone would see the ugliness. It was powerful, and it spoke to the very core of me. I was familiar with that walk, but instead of dragging my burdens behind me, I carried them deep within. I was transfixed because I felt like that woman in the skit was me. Though out of sight from others, things like unmet expectations, regret, bitterness, envy, dreams collecting dust, fears, anger, shame, and unforgiveness held a huge space within me.

Does this sound familiar to you? If you took a careful look in the mirror, would you see in your reflection some of those carefully tended burdens held tightly to you? I know you didn't pick them up on purpose. It wasn't like you planned this, but here you are carrying things from year to year, from relationship to relationship, while the layers keep heaping up, more chains shackled to you...holding you back, holding you imprisoned – stuck.

You are not alone. In Genesis 19:26, we find Lot and his wife literally running for their very lives. They were promised safe-keeping with one simple instruction: to not look back. The scripture passage shares with us the outcome, "Lot's wife looked back, and she became a pillar of salt." Like most of us, Lot's wife was not able to let go, and the consequence was dire. Maybe you resemble Lot's wife, hardened... paralyzed... stuck.

Are you exhausted from trying to hold it all together? Do you feel like you could use a reset as you begin this new year? You can choose to allow God to not only heal you but transform you. You can live a life free from this load. A life that does not gaze upon the dead things. A life that does not hold onto the very things that are robbing you of living free of the past. One that instead looks forward to the things that bring assurance and freedom. It is not simple, but it is a battle that can be won. It is a battle worth fighting with all you've got because it is for your very life! Can you imagine living a life free, no longer stuck, no longer carrying around burdens that have piled up through the years? This year can be the year that not only turns the calendar page but also the year that you write a new chapter in your story.

Quite possibly, it has been the mental battle that has weighed you down. Our thought patterns are crazy powerful! We have been told so many lies about ourselves. It can be difficult to separate our own thoughts from the opinions of others that we have taken on. In Romans 12:2 we read, "Do not conform to the pattern of this world, but be transformed by the renewing of your mind." Does this resonate with you? In this new year, do you feel like you could use a little renewal?

It is important when engaging in battle to not only arm yourself but to know your enemy. It is vital to know what Satan is using to attack you. Satan is the master deceiver, the basis of all lies, and the destroyer of relationships. He revels in our mistakes, fertilizes temptation, and stirs up unforgiveness, anger, and hatred. What are the weapons that Satan uses against you?

Bring them out into the open. It is powerful to confess them to God. One of mine would be, "You are too old." I am in this season where people my age are beginning to look towards retiring. I don't want to retire. I don't want to sit on the sidelines. I have learned to combat those negative thoughts with positive ones. Throughout history, God has used more "seasoned" people to do His work. My positive thought has become: *who am I to determine God's timing?* If God is not limited by age, then neither will I be!

Maybe your struggle is more along the lines of a spiritual battle. For years, I struggled with shame, and I believed that God should <u>not</u> forgive me. Can you relate? Do you know the tentacles of shame, the mistakes whispered to you in the dark, holding you captive? Take heart! Scripture is filled with people who completely messed things up. They all suffered the consequences of their mistakes, but for those who repented and confessed, they found an even better relationship with God. In Psalm 103:3-4, we find David praising God for that very wondrous reality: "Praise the LORD, O my soul, and forget not all his benefits; who forgives all your sins and heals all your diseases, who redeems your life from the pit and crowns you with love and compassion; who satisfies your desires with good things, so that your youth is renewed like the eagles."

This, by far, is one of my favorite passages of Scripture! What a mind and heart change! David is testifying to the truth that God can take a life that is buried in a pit of sin and disease and redeem it! I was that person. At one time, I lived very far from God, but because of His grace and mercy, I no longer do. What God did for me, He can also do for you. Do you have any unconfessed sin lingering around? Are you buried in a pit? God wants good things for you. He loves you deeply, passionately without limits! He purposefully and with great intention created you to be one of His children, chosen to be an instrument of His grace and mercy to a world that is starved for Him. Instead of bitterness, anger, or regret clogging up your heart, this is the year, the day to focus on what God is offering, and you, too, can experience that same heart change. I encourage you to stop right here and take some time, sit at the feet of Jesus, and have a good old heart-to-heart with Him.

This is a journey. It is not simple, but it is not one that we go alone. In Matthew 11: 28-30, Jesus offers all of us this beautiful invitation, "Come to me, all you who are weary and burdened, and I will give you rest. Take my yoke upon you and learn from me, for I am gentle and humble in heart, and you will find rest for your souls. For my yoke is easy and my burden is light." Every time I read those verses, I inhale deeply and exhale even deeper.

Jesus doesn't expect us to have all the answers, to always have it all together, or to not make mistakes. Jesus knows we are going to mess up. He knows that we are going to have bad days. He also knows that we are never going to get where we need to go if we don't go with Him. He knows this world will mislead us, chew us up, and spit us out—that's why this invitation is so powerful. Jesus used this analogy of yoked oxen to let us know that the invitation is for us, but once we accept it, we will never be alone. When two oxen are yoked together, it is not two equal oxen that are yoked. There is one stronger, more experienced ox yoked to a less experienced ox. The younger ox learns from the other while the stronger ox pulls the heavier load.

Jesus knows you have some tender, fragile places buried deep inside of you. Trust His gentleness. Trust His forgiveness. Trust His guidance. Trust His love for you! Jesus bears the weight so that we can walk in freedom!

It is possible to walk in freedom, to set those things down and grab hold of life with both hands without looking back. It isn't so much about changing the superficial things but instead allowing God to heal us from the inside out. God cares deeply if your heart is weighed down by such things like unforgiveness, shame, anger, jealousy, and regret. It is those things that are insidious to all areas of our lives.

One of the most important gifts that we can give ourselves is the gift of quiet space. A time to reflect so that our souls can find rest. The following are some practical steps that you can take this new year. Although they are not a magical formula and-poof!-all is well, there are steps designed to help you lay it all down and open yourself up to what God can do. Take some time to sit with your journal and consider the following as you take a new direction this new year.

- You have to get right with God. Without doing that, you will not make any healthy movement forward. If you did not do so earlier, confess to God what you are struggling with. Identify what you have been carrying around. You might be able to hide it from everyone else, but you cannot hide it from God. He has always known. He is just waiting for you to share it with Him because confession opens the door to forgiveness and freedom. If you are floundering for the words, it may help to pray David's prayer found in Psalm 139:23-24, "Search me, God, and know my heart; test me and know my anxious thoughts. See if there is any offensive way in me, and lead me in the way everlasting."
- This can be scary but trust the process. Grab a full sheet of paper and draw a grid (much like a tic-tac-toe board) on it. It is even okay to start out with just a few squares. This is your battle plan, so make it your own. Write out some of the negative thought patterns you have. Place one in each square of the grid. If you can only write in one square, that is great! I applaud your bravery. As one negative thought pattern is conquered, you can add more at that time.
- For example, In your first square, you may write, "God isn't going to forgive me for my past mistakes."
- In each square, underneath the negative thought,

write out an opposite positive thought. This will be difficult. You are retraining your brain. It may help to write it on a post-it note and then place it over your negative thought.

- For example: Underneath the negative thought, "God isn't going to forgive me for my past mistakes," you could write something like, "Jesus died to forgive me and is faithful to forgive my sins."
- Research Scripture and see what God's Word says about either the positive or negative thoughts. When a verse resonates with you, write it down. Make sure to thank God for speaking to you through His Word. His Word is so good! Don't be dismayed if a scripture does not jump out at you right away. Part of the healing process is to trust God with the timing. Know He is faithful!
- For example: After you have written out "God isn't going to forgive me for my past mistakes" and corrected it with the truth, "Jesus died to forgive me and is faithful to forgive my every sin," underneath that, you would write a scripture, "He has removed our sins as far from us as the east is from the west" (Psalm 103:12, NLT).
- What are the good things that God is telling you through Scripture? What is He revealing to you in His Word? Embrace those things and pray over them. Use your grid as a reminder to focus your prayers. Praying God's Word keeps us in alignment with God, and it will slowly begin to change our hearts. Hold onto the truth!

- Prepare for war and remember that a war is not won quickly or easily. It is going to require you to be strategic, diligent, and prepared. When doubt creeps in, or an arrow from Satan finds its mark, you are going to do battle with the truth of what God has revealed to you by praying it out, claiming God's truth!
- Repeat! Here is the reality. As soon as one of our broken layers is healed another will be revealed and need some tending to. Sin is a part of every one of our lives, and we are all broken. We have to be intentional about peeling the layers back to make sure we are not picking up another burden we were never meant to carry.

I have made many mistakes, and for a long time, they stuck to me like glue. It gave Satan quite the playground to dance around in. I would be driving down the road to the grocery store, and–kapow–there would be this arrow of Satan puncturing my peace of mind, and off my thought patterns would go. When I didn't have the words to pray, I would use the strongest weapon I know: the name of Jesus. I would declare that the Word of God tells me that Satan cannot stand in the presence of Jesus, and over and over AND over again, I would proclaim the name of Jesus! Until my mind was once again consumed by what I was saying and not on the arrows that Satan was zinging my way. Freedom.

A new year. A time to reflect. A time to embrace all that God offers. Freedom is a beautiful thing, but only those who find their identity in Jesus know what freedom really is. Don't live stuck, don't live with a lie, and don't live with a false identity. You can walk in freedom, and you can let go of that load you have been carrying. Your heavenly Father longs for you to live this big, beautiful life with your eyes focused on Him. Your vision no longer clouded by yesterday, but instead moving forward. Unashamed. Unshackled. Unburdened.

About the Authors

Natalie d'Aubermont Thompson

Natalie d'Aubermont Thompson lives outside Ann Arbor, Michigan, with her husband David, their three rapidly growing children, and their super-pup, Patches. She's the founder/CEO of Saltar Consulting, where she focuses on leadership coaching and organizational development. She also writes about all things literary-related at Living by the Page. Natalie is Argentine-American and has worked, studied, and volunteered in over 40 countries. She received her BA from Tufts University and her Master's from the London School of Economics in International Relations.

Connect with Natalie:

www.livingbythepage.com

About the Authors

Brianna Johnson

As a special needs mom, Brianna Johnson is an expert at balancing multiple priorities and parenting in the best way for each of her three sons, even when that looks drastically different. Those same skills that make her a better mom make her a better manager and coach. With 20 years of experience in human resources and corporate communications, she has developed training and programs on a variety of topics, all with the goal of making communication clearer and more consistent so that teams can be more effective and successful together.

Connect with Brianna:

www.briannajohnson.com

Rebecca McCartney, LCSW

Rebecca McCartney is a therapist who provides online counseling to women in Texas and Tennessee. Rebecca serves Christian women by honoring and incorporating faith into the care she provides. She is trauma-trained and educates and supports women with a history of trauma. She specializes in working with women who are anxious and overwhelmed. Rebecca helps women better understand the source of emotional pain, teaches coping skills, and works with clients to develop a path toward growth and healing. She lives in Houston, Texas, with her husband and two teenage sons.

Connect with Rebecca:

rebeccamccartneylcsw.com

Facebook: https://www.facebook.com/RebeccaMcCartneyLCSW

Jennifer Gorham, Psy.D.

Jennifer has a personal passion for integrating psychology with faith and theology for the purpose of developing a spiritually formed life and healthy faith communities. She earned her doctorate in psychology from Wheaton College in Illinois and currently has a private practice where she primarily focuses on anxiety and trauma. A Southern transplant to New England, Jennifer has lived in Massachusetts for ten years with her husband of twenty-two years and two teenagers. She serves in her local church in a number of ways, including leading the prayer ministry.

Connect with Jennifer:

Instagram: @drjennifergorham

Rehana De Villiers

*R*ehana De Villiers, originally from South Africa, lives in Columbia, South Carolina, with her husband and two adult children. In Africa are her three bonus children and grandchildren, whom she wishes lived closer. A corporate professional by day, Rehana's passion is women's discipleship. Raised in a Muslim home, she considers it a blessed privilege to have attended seminary and is burdened for all women to know sound theology to deepen and mature their own and others' faith. She loves to speak to women about Jesus, the cornerstone of her hope. This is her second contribution to a collaborative book project.

Connect with Rehana:
Facebook: Rehana De Villiers

Lindsay Koach

Lindsay is a wife and mother of three children, an Integrative Nutrition health coach, and a Naturopathic Practitioner specializing in women's thyroid and hormone health. She was born and raised and resides with her family in Ellwood City, Pennsylvania. In addition to in-person health coaching, she offers an online course for thyroid healing and a hypothyroidism support group on Facebook. You can find more information on her course, as well as articles and other written works, on her website, heartspeakhealth.com.

Connect with Lindsay:

https://www.heartspeakhealth.com

Facebook and Instagram: @heartspeakhealth

A Peaceful New Year

Melissa Manion

Melissa Manion likes to say she stumbled her way to Jesus. Her life was far from perfect, but on the day she realized God could make beauty from ashes, everything changed. Since then, she has been writing and speaking to the broken and hurting in hopes that they will know that no one is ever too far gone to receive God's love. Her words are a balm for the weary soul. You can find her anywhere there is a shoreline, sipping on iced coffee, pondering this one crazy life! She is a proud wife to Jeremy, mother to five children (one home with Jesus), and Gigi to one. A Massachusetts girl living in Connecticut, Melissa is a New Englander to her core!

Connect with Melissa:

boastingaboutmyweaknesses.blogspot.com

MelissaManion.com

Facebook: Melissa Manion

Instagram: melissa.n.manion

About the Authors

Nancy Radloff

Nancy Radloff served as a teacher for 39 years with a passion to let her students see Jesus! Raised in Milwaukee, Wisconsin, she graduated from Concordia University-Wisconsin, earned a Masters in Education from Aurora University-Illinois, and taught in three states. Throughout her teaching ministry, Nancy provided elementary students and many adults with easy-to-use, interactive Bible study approaches. In addition to classroom teaching, she has mentored teachers, presented workshops, and coached writers, equipping others in their purpose. Nancy and her husband, Mark, live in northern Wisconsin, where you will find her writing, coaching writers, and kayaking.

Connect with Nancy:

www.nancylradloff.com

Facebook: Nancy Radloff Writer

Instagram: @nancylradloff

Jess Henning

*J*ess Henning is a wife to her high school sweetheart and momma of four boys. She loves helping authors and creative entrepreneurs launch their books and build their brands with clarity and confidence. As a Certified hope*writers Coach and Certified StoryBrand Coach, Jess has a deep passion for making marketing simple and accessible. She empowers her clients through personalized coaching, strategic brand and website design, and actionable courses. When she's not writing, Jess loves hanging out with her boys in the great outdoors.

Connect with Jess:

www.jesshenning.com

Instagram: @jesshenning.co.

About the Authors

Stephanie Gavel

Stephanie and her husband, Ron, of three years, live in Beaver, PA. Stephanie has four adult children: two sons and two daughters. She will tell you that parenting has been one of the greatest blessings that God could have ever given her. With her children grown, Stephanie is writing her second act, where she is following the call that God placed on her heart years ago, which was to write. It is her great desire to share the truth of God with those who need to hear it the most: the lost, the broken, the weary, and the battered. She is active in her church through a young adult discipling ministry, teaching adult classes, and developing a foster care ministry. One of her favorite scripture passages is Psalm 103, especially verses 2-4, "Praise the LORD, O my soul, and forget not all his benefits—who forgives all your sins and heals all your diseases, who redeems your life from the pit and crowns you with love and compassion." She believes that every life can be redeemed because no pit is too big that God cannot pull you out of if only we surrender our mess to Him. You can find her blog posts on bythepottershand.com.

Connect with Stephanie:

www.bythepottershand.com

Dear Reader,

Thank you for reading A *Peaceful New Year*

I want to take a moment to celebrate the incredible authors who contributed to this meaningful book. They have poured their hearts into discovering, clarifying, and sharing their unique messages—and now, you get to benefit from their hard work and dedication.

At hope*books, we are deeply proud of our authors and are honored to partner with them on this journey. If you've ever considered writing and publishing your book, we invite you to visit hopebooks.com to learn more about our coaching and publishing services. We believe that everyone has a message to share and an audience to serve, and the world needs your hopeful words now more than ever.

Once again, let's take a moment to celebrate the hard work of these authors in bringing A *Peaceful New Year* to life.

Sincerely,

Brian Dixon

Publisher, hope*books

Looking to *connect* with a community of writers?

hope*writers
www.hopewriters.com

The world needs your *hope-filled* words more now than ever before.

Thinking about *writing* your own book?

hope*books
www.hopebooks.com